Let Go of

The Hope Cha

Trust in the Lord and do good. Then you will live safely in the land and prosper. Take delight in the Lord and he will give you your heart's desires. Everything you do to the Lord. Trust him, and he will help you. He will make your innocence as clear as the dawn, and the justice of your cause will shine like the noonday sun.

Psalm 37:3–6 (NLT)

Let Go of the Ring

Ralph Moore

Straight Street Publishing
Honolulu, Hawaii

Published by Straight Street Publishing, a ministry of Hope Chapel
Kaneohe, P.O. Box 240041, Honolulu, HI 96824-00041, Tel. (800)
711-9369 toll-free, (808) 235-5814
www.hopechapel.com

Cover design by O Communications and Darlene O.S. Ching

Library of Congress Cataloging-in-Publication Data
Moore, Ralph
    Let Go of the Ring / Ralph Moore with Dan Beach
        Includes: illustrations, photographs.
        ISBN 0-9628127-2-4
        Fourth edition
        1. Moore, Ralph. 2. Clergy—Biography.
        3. Christian biography. 4. Hope Chapel (Kaneohe, Hawaii).
        5. Evangelistic work—United States. 6. Evangelicalism.
        I. Beach. Dan. II. Title.
        BR1725.M667.A3 2000   289.9-dc20

Printed in the United States of America
00 01 02 03 04   10 9 8 7 6 5 4 3 2

A Word of Thanks

Our rewards in this life reflect our treasures in heaven. Human relations are the best of God's gifts during our earthly walk. This book is not the story of one man, but the faith-journey of thousands of interlocking friendships. Without these people's clear-eyed, courageous intent to please God, the events in this book would not have happened. This story reflects the lives of some pretty great people, my wonderful friends and family. I've intentionally "name-dropped" wherever possible. I want the right people to get the credit for "the Hope Chapel story."

At the heart of my journey are those closest to me. Ruby, my patient and trusting wife, keeps me standing. Our children Carl and Kelly stand strong in the Lord and give testimony to God's grace in a rising generation. These are my rewards.

Contents

1   Let Go of the Ring   9

2   Choices   13

3   On-the-Job Training   27

4   Going, Going, Gone   35

5   Reaching Out   53

6   Love and Unity   75

7   Filled and Overflowing   85

8   MiniChurch   103

Illustration: Early Church Architecture   111

9   Vision   117

10   Give 'Em Heaven   139

11   Church on the Beach   151

12   Building Bridges   163

13   Taking the Land   179

14   Growing to Maturity   199

15   Like a Coconut Tree   219

Illustration: Coconut Tree   223

1

LET GO OF THE RING

"You'll never let go of the ring, Frodo, they never do."

My friend Ken Hiroshige is a dentist. He had me where I couldn't escape, pinned down in that big chair, mouth propped open, his hands deftly working a very long needle into my jaw.

"They never let go when they get to your place. It just isn't done. There is too much pride involved. You'd have to really sell out and I don't think you can."

In J.R.R. Tolkien's splendid trilogy, *The Lord of the Rings,* a hobbit named Frodo (a small, human-like forest creature) is faced with a dilemma. He possesses a ring that can give him control over the whole world. But at the same time it can corrupt the owner and turn him into a despot. If he destroys the ring, a godly order will be restored to the world, but he will be left powerless. If he retains it, he can rule and take his chances with the moral corruption that accompanies the power of the ring.

You'll have to read *The Lord of the Rings* to find out what Frodo did; this is a story about what happened to me.

I had just told my friend Ken that I felt God calling me to leave my very secure job of 10 years to start a church in another city, involving people of an entirely different racial and cultural background. It meant leaving the pastorate of a congregation of more than 2,000 people and a home in a California beach town that fit like my own skin. I'd be leaving friends who I dearly loved. All this at a time when my church was becoming the focus of incredible attention in the local and national media.

The Associated Press had just put out a story about our church that ran on radio stations and in newspapers across the country. Now the TV networks were doing follow-up interviews. We were even written up in *Esquire* magazine. It was pretty heavy stuff to leave behind for the relative obscurity of a pioneer pastorate, in a distant city where I knew practically no one.

Ken was right. It would be difficult to leave the security that I knew for the insecurity of a pioneer relocation. However, he was wrong.

LOSING TO GAIN

The Bible is loaded with stories of people who have let go of the "ring" in their lives. The ring, as Ken spoke of it, represents power, position, and prominence. More importantly, it represents *control* of our lives. All the things we cling to for security are things that God wants to disrupt. We must learn to let go of those things, lay down our life, pick up our cross and follow Jesus. Christianity works best in the tension of letting go so we can receive—of seeking to lose our life so we can find it.

God called Abraham to leave his father's house, his idols, his friends, the familiarity of his circumstances, the promise of his father's inheritance, and political power. God told him to get up, leave his father's house and go looking for a land that he would show him.

The Lord didn't tell Abraham where he was going or what he was going to find. He didn't describe the geography or introduce him to any of the people along the way. He simply said, "Leave this place behind and go into a land that I'll show you." He didn't even give him a map.

But he did promise to bless Abraham if he had the guts to trust him, letting go of all human touches of security.

After Abraham left his father's house, God started to define the blessing. God promised that he would give him a son. He promised that he would, through that son, make a nation of people. He pledged that, through this new nation, all the world would be blessed. He assured him that he would go with him; that anyone who would bless Abraham, God would bless; and anyone who would curse Abraham, God would curse.

Abraham was called to let go of the ring and trust God, to walk by faith and not by sight. I believe that God calls us all to live that way.

As you move through the Scriptures, you come upon Moses forsaking the riches of Egypt to serve God. You find Daniel abandoning potential success in the king's house by eating the way God commanded in the Law. You discover young Jeremiah leaving his occupation and Amos selling his fig farm to go serve the Lord. Shadrach, Meshach, and Abednego not only let go of the ring of power and position in Babylon, they laid their lives on the line when they refused to worship the statue of the king.

FOLLOW ME . . .

In the New Testament, we encounter Jesus at the desk of a wealthy businessman. He looked Matthew straight in the face and said, "Follow me." There was no definition, no direction. He didn't promise to make him an apostle. He didn't let him know that he was to become a best-selling author. He only said, "Follow me."

Matthew was in immediate jeopardy. Every relationship, everything he possessed, his stature in the community was all up for grabs. Without anything to cling to but trust, he let go of the ring, and he followed after the Lord.

Letting go is hard. But it's the only way to success. As I think back on my life, I've faced the same dilemma as Matthew and Abraham. I've been asked to let go of that ring of control and security. I remember a time when I was still very young. . . .

2

CHOICES

The crisis came when I was about to enter my senior year of high school. However, the dilemma really started when I was about six-years-old.

That occasion was the first time I can remember any direct communication from the Lord, and it wasn't very pleasant. I was standing at the top of the staircase where we lived. My infant brother in the bedroom across the hall let out a horrible scream; my sister must have pinched him.

As my Dad mounted the stairs he told my mother, "With those lungs that kid ought to be a preacher." (This event came on the heels of my father wanting to move us from Portland to Los Angeles in order to go to Bible school so he could preach). I hated the idea. It meant leaving my school, my friends and all that.) My father's next words were, "Gosh, I wish one of my boys would wind up being a pastor some day."

Something inside of me screamed, "It'll be him, not me! I never want to be a preacher!" From that day on I knew (I can't explain *how* I knew, but I knew) God had spoken to me through my Dad. I rebelled inside. As much as a little kid can get angry, I was angry.

For the next 13 years I fought with the memory of that day. I would never really serve the Lord because I knew that to let go all the way meant being a preacher, and I wanted to be an architect. I went all through high school rebelling against God's call to pastor.

I went to church, prayed and read the Bible, but lived like the devil at school with my friends. My friends and I went to camp every year and disrupted the place. Once we fed laxatives to a kitten and let it loose in a church service. Another time we cut off the electric power while they were washing dishes and getting ready to start church. The pranks went on and on.

At one particular meeting I filled a huge hypodermic syringe with water. During prayer I shot all that water at the ceiling and we had rain. However funny it was, I felt sick at myself for having done it. I told a close friend that I was tired of being a two-faced Christian. He felt the same way, and we made a decision to end our double-minded lifestyle.

Our plan was to read 10 chapters of the Bible a day for 30 days and then to come to a decision. We would either serve the Lord consistently or get out of church and really taste the "delights of the world" which, for two 17-year-old boys, mostly meant women.

I read 300 chapters of the Bible and could not escape the Spirit-filled life that came with it. I committed myself to do whatever God asked. The problem was that I already knew what he wanted. He had asked when I was only six.

I was 17 and faced with a dilemma. If I was really going to follow the Lord, I was going to have to do what he said. But I didn't want to be a pastor; I wanted to be an architect.

I was in a college architectural program at my high school. A couple of small buildings that I designed had been built, and I felt fairly successful at a very early age. I didn't want to let go of all that. Those things may not seem consequential to you, but for a 17-year-old, it was my whole world.

LETTING GO

The ring is hard to release. Not only was I faced with the dilemma of changing careers, there were other costs as well. There were my friends, most of whom opposed my decision. The night before I left Portland to go to Bible college in Los Angeles, a friend of mine took me to a restaurant where he spent two hours trying to convince me that I was making a mistake and that it was going to cost our friendship. My employer pulled me aside, telling me that I should pursue a business major in a local university and then move on to architecture. He was even willing to help finance my education if I would stay in Portland. My parents weren't sure that I was making the right decision. I remember leaving my girlfriend, knowing that my decision would cost me the hope of ever marrying her.

Whatever I had that could please me—architecture, security, money, influence in the community—all of that had to be passed aside. I had to let go of the ring, lay down my life, take up my cross and follow Jesus.

A LIFE SENTENCE

I entered LIFE Bible College in the fall of 1965. I really enjoyed it for the first few weeks. Then I began grabbing for that old ring.

At first it was exciting to be in Los Angeles. I enjoyed the fast pace, the endless summer, even the city itself. Those were the days when the glory of Los Angeles was just beginning to fade. We were encountering the drug revolution and campus rebellion, but there was still the security of the easy-living '50s and early '60s which became subject matter for all those Beach Boys songs.

Los Angeles was a good place to live. On top of that, college was loads of fun. We would stage fake fights in the dorms. One time some guys started a fake fight out in the street in front of the school in order to upset the neighbor ladies. Another student called the cops on them, and we all had a good laugh. There were a lot of other pranks and all the good times that makes college a great experience for a young person.

It was during those days that I met my wife, Ruby. I had little money, so we became great friends by going for walks in the park or riding the bus to the beach.

After several joyous months, frustration set in. I didn't really like the school. The college was small, its recent graduates hadn't really accomplished a great deal, and it had self-inflicted insecurities. The school was a class act offering solid professors and a wonderful biblical foundation. The problem arose from constant comparisons to other, more secular, Christian colleges. These comparisons resulted in a lot of busy work for our student body.

What I considered silly routines and meaningless rituals were forced on us, while real class work was not as challenging as I had expected. The school certainly did not measure up to my rather immature expectations. I knew the history of LIFE Bible College and the exploits of its early graduates. They stood in stark contrast to the school as I found it.

The college even imposed a dress code. We weren't allowed to wear Levis or shorts. To protest, some of us wore clothes that fit the dress code, but never changed them. One time I went for a whole month wearing the same two shirts on alternating days.

I was very depressed about the whole situation. Teachers would give assignments, but nobody would do their homework on time. Diligent students were penalized by teachers giving extra time when others cried on due day. I started writing notes on the top of my papers in red ink, grading the teacher on her performance with the homework before I turned it in.

It became frustrating for me, and I began to wish that I had gone to the University of Oregon or Stanford. I found myself looking for another Bible college to attend and sent away for catalogs from every school I could find in my first year.

I even remember one day when the dorm manager stopped us from playing catch with a softball because he said that Sunday was the Sabbath. The whole school seemed silly to me. But my responses to it were immature. I chaffed against everything around me. God constantly reassured me I was in the right place, but I continued to rebel at my circumstances. Since then I've found that you grow fastest in humbling situations, but at the time I didn't understand. As a result, I sinned by my poor attitude.

IRONING OUT SOME WRINKLES

Paul writes in Romans 13 that rulers and authorities are established by God. He says we are to submit. As we do, our pride is usually injured. We lose control to the Lord and those in authority over us. Outwardly the situation can look hopeless, but God seems to use the peripheral elements of a situation to bless us.

Let me tell you how it worked for me.

LIFE Bible College was like God's steam iron taking a couple of prideful wrinkles out of my life. Beyond that, the school blessed me in many ways, although I was too immature to notice at the time. During the time I was in school, I met and married my wife. I was also fortunate to be tutored by a fantastic educator, Dr. Dorothy Jean Furlong. Any ability I have to teach and maintain a rapport with an audience is a gift of the Holy Spirit bestowed through my association with this tough-minded, yet sensitive and challenging woman.

I became good friends with a man named Jack Hayford who today pastors a congregation called The Church on the Way. Jack had a strong imprint on my life. He was director of the youth program for the Foursquare denomination and his office was near our campus. He befriended and coached me through a lot of my struggles in those years.

There was another very important woman who became a tower in my life—Eloise Clarno, who worked as director of Sunday Schools for the denomination. She listened endlessly to my complaints and frustrations, always encouraging me to press on and keep on track.

I went to school to get an education, assuming I would get it all in the classroom. I didn't understand that my being in the school afforded relationships with people who God was using to shape me into a pastor. The entire faculty consisted of godly, dedicated people. Though the school was going through times of transition, their healthy example marked every student.

We were required to attend chapel every Friday, and I hated it. To me, it was just a poor excuse for church, and I was already involved in a great church. However, in one chapel service, we were taught by a man named Barney Northcoat who had planted a church about 20 years earlier. It had grown from just a handful of people up to a congregation of considerable size. His story and spark of adventure made a remarkable impression on my life. I sat and listened and felt the adrenaline flow through my body like never before. I listened to this man share his fears and failures as he had built his church.

Something good bit me that day; it seemed that God indicated Barney's experience was to be my own. That delighted me. In school I often listened to other students discussing their desires to go out and pastor upon graduation (you have to understand that LIFE Bible College is basically a "pastor factory"). Classmates would covet this pulpit or another one. Some were already beginning to shine the old apple as they hoped to work their way into some of the larger pulpits of America. I was angry at all this covetous talk, and Barney Northcoat presented a godly alternative.

LEARNING BY DOING

LIFE Bible College required all students to work in a church as a volunteer, ministering to people. You could teach Sunday School or work with a youth group, even preaching in a convalescent hospital. The choice was ours, but whatever it was, we had to get some kind of practical experience. Whatever I might have felt about the system, the overall effect was beneficial to me. It thrust me in-to the ministry.

I found myself involved in a tiny church in the San Fernando Valley in a place called Granada Hills. Many of the families had just moved away as a result of an industry-wide aerospace layoff. Art Miller, the new pastor, found himself left with about 35 people on his first Sunday.

Art came to the dorm on my first Sunday in the college, trying to recruit my gregarious, talented roommate to work with him. My roommate, Thom Whitaker, turned him down. Thom was a whiz kid with much to offer. I felt very embarrassed and untalented as I asked Art if it would be okay if I came to his church. You have to understand that for me to go to this church, Art would have to provide transportation. He'd have to drive a 70-mile round trip each Sunday, in addition to all his other pastoral responsibilities. Seventy miles was a good deal considering Thom with all his talents, but I was no Thom Whitaker. He said yes, and I ended up recruiting eight other people. So nine of us crammed into a station wagon each Sunday to help get the church off the ground.

For me, it was almost a church-planting exercise and I was able to learn the ropes of building something out of nothing. We never had enough finances and yet God always met the needs of that congregation.

I learned a fantastic lesson on a day when the men of the church were adding on a section to the auditorium. They had torn away much of the roof and an outside wall in order to mount a steel I-beam in the structure. The hot August afternoon broke up in a freak thundershower that threatened the exposed interior of the building. Not only would carpet and furniture be ruined, but electrical junctions would be exposed to water.

Instead of rushing to the roof with yards of plastic tarp, those men got on their knees and prayed. The storms passed us by. There was rain around all sides of the property but none on our lot. I was overwhelmed by their faith and by the Lord's response.

A TURNING POINT

At a youth rally in our church just prior to the end of my freshman year, I met a young man named Jerry Cook. He had just graduated from Fuller Theological Seminary and had served as youth pastor in the Foursquare church in La Puente, where my wife grew up.

I had a good rapport with Jerry. He was only 25 and was headed to pastor a tiny church located about four miles from my parent's house in a little town called Gresham, Oregon. I accompanied him in the venture. I had heard him speak in late May and got all excited about his vision. We arrived in town in the latter part of June, and I was able to attend his first Sunday as pastor.

The congregation had existed for more than 10 years. When Jerry arrived along with me and a couple of friends, the grand total of the congregation was 28. These people had been together for all this time but there had been no real leadership. They met in an ancient wooden church building, with a parsonage next door. Someone had set the parsonage on fire burning off most of the roof and second story. The city condemned the building, but left it standing. It just perched there looking very ugly. The congregation leased the whole property for $1 a year. The financial break couldn't compensate for the poor quality.

Without leadership and laboring in substandard facilities, these were demoralized people. In effect, Jerry Cook was a church planter who suffered the misfortune of inheriting an unresolved history. It would have been easier to start with nothing.

I was fortunate to watch Jerry's mistakes and successes in those first few months. Throughout the summer he preached on the First Letter of John, concentrating on the love of God. He taught of God's care for us. Jerry's quiet confidence and unflappable smile built confidence and hope in the tiny congregation. Jerry changed the name to Easthill Church. Word got around and the church began to grow. That church would eventually grow to number more than six thousand people.

I taught a Sunday school class, made up of people ages 12-36. It wasn't exactly your typical junior high class. We had a great time until we experienced a tragedy late in that summer. A young man in that class accidentally blew the back of his head off with a shot gun. He had been playing around and showing off for his friends at the gas station where he worked. He put what he thought was an empty shot gun in his mouth and pulled the trigger. The night before the accident, someone had loaded the gun. The tragedy was horrifying, but I was learning from Jerry how to handle shocking circumstances.

The denomination soon put money down on a building that had belonged to another church group. They believed in Jerry and invested money to prove it. About 10 weeks into his pastorate, the church moved to the new facility.

One day I was out weeding the church yard and God spoke to me. He reinforced what he had said that day in chapel and told me that I had been allowed to work with Art Miller and

Jerry Cook because I was going to be a church planter. I was frightened, but thrilled with the challenge.

STUDENT BODY PRESIDENT

Back at school, someone finally called my bluff regarding my stinky attitude toward college. I was receiving a good education both in and out of the classroom, but I was still quite obnoxious. I was feeling secure enough to get pretty loud about my opinions. I began to sound off about policy around the school.

By my senior year Jack Hayford was now on the faculty both as an instructor and dean of students. He worked hard to improve the faculty and had plans to build a prayer chapel for the students.

My friend and I felt that we needed a student center a lot more than we needed a new prayer chapel, since we already had a small prayer room on campus. The priority for a student center was very real since LIFE Bible College was then located in Echo Park, a really tough Los Angeles neighborhood. Off campus, fraternizing was very difficult, and the three-acre campus didn't offer too much space for student activity. We began to lobby and rally for a student center and some vacant classroom space.

I found myself bouncing off of other people's feelings. Frankly, I was causing a lot of trouble. One day Jack called me into his office. He told me I was a rabble rouser and pressed me to get more involved in the normal channels of student government. We had a four-hour talk that afternoon, and he made a lot of sense to me. However, at some point I decided I wasn't going to get involved. I would back off and leave everyone alone; let them do their thing and keep my mouth shut.

A few weeks went by and student elections were due. I received a phone call from Jack, asking me why I hadn't had the *courage* to run for student office. The school had recently changed its government and had upgraded the positions of the student body officers. Fresh input was now possible.

I shrugged my shoulders and said I wasn't interested. He reminded me that I always had plenty to say. He suggested I ought to put my money where my mouth was. I still remember walking to the campus that Saturday morning to fill out the petition to run for student body president.

The election came off in a tie. I had run against two of my best friends and faced an old roommate in the runoff. Somehow, I won.

I was very surprised. It was the first time that I had ever really gotten involved in school. I'd been hanging onto that ring of protection and control. You can't stay in control if you take chances with things like elections.

I gave my best. Four of us—Allona Ellithorpe (Eastland), Dale Downs, Donna Tallent, and myself put three hours a day on top of our studies and jobs. Because of the new Student Body Constitution, we literally invented our roles in student government.

It was one of those sideline educations God had for me. I was still in an institution that I hadn't fully grown to appreciate and yet God was blessing me with another surprise education. My role as student body president stretched me and taught me to lead large numbers of people. I learned valuable lessons that cannot be taught in a classroom. As I look back, I only regret that I wasn't open to make better use of all four years in that college. I was simply too prideful and too worried about staying in the driver's seat to make the best of it.

A LITTLE TOO SMART!

By the time that I was ready to graduate from LIFE Bible College, I was feeling pretty secure, almost cocky. My experience as student body president had been a very good one. We had rallied the students to attend social events and ball games to the degree where we had 80 percent involvement. The Student Body Treasury tripled in one year and we created a "student body building fund" for the school that was able to generate enough money to construct *both* the student center *and* chapel in a couple of surplus classrooms. Things generally flourished, and it all went to my head.

I changed jobs a lot while I was in college, moving from a part-time job when I had a heavy schedule in the fall, to a full-time job in the spring. This way, I could make some money and keep myself afloat financially.

In my last quarter I had a pretty cushy part-time job at the *Los Angeles Times*. I walked into the personnel office and asked the director for a job. When he asked what I could do, I looked him straight in the eye (trembling inside), and said I could do any part-time job better than anybody else in the place. I wrote out an application including a reference from Brunswick Bowling Corporation where I had earned journeyman carpenter's wages for two summers. This man was very impressed that anybody would pay me that much money at my tender age. I then told him about my schedule and refused any jobs interfering with classes or my schedule as student body president. I think he mistook my arrogance for self confidence because he worked hard to find a position that would meet my needs.

The job he came up with was really something. Mostly we did customer relations work, but my position included a strange twist. Every day for an hour and a half, I put on a white shirt and tie and delivered newspapers on a little chrome cart. I had an *executive* newspaper route; I delivered the late final edition to Otis Chandler, editor-in-chief of the newspaper. I was pretty impressed with all that went on in the building—the way they operated, the pride that everyone took in their jobs. But more than that I was impressed with myself.

I thought I was hot stuff, rubbing shoulders with those people. It created pride and caused me to try to slip out of the timing the Lord had for my life. I was going to run out and plant churches, right then. Although the church in Granada Hills had offered me a very good job with adequate pay upon graduation, I decided to back out and go set the world afire for Jesus at age 22. I was taking the ring back into my hands.

College graduation and a little company experience led me to believe that I was ready for anything. In reality, my education was far from complete. The Lord had more training in store for me. Besides, he needed time to create the right environment in the place he was calling me to serve.

3

ON-THE-JOB TRAINING

It is easy to get ahead of God. You start with a sense of calling, add some legitimate success, toss in a new vision and you can become pretty self important. At least, I did.

Pride leads to destruction, even if it is wrapped in spirituality and a sense of mission. But God is gracious and willing to block the pathway to folly. His plans work because they include unseen elements that we could never understand or anticipate. Our plans will, at best, be limited to human understanding. At worst, they will be crafted in arrogance and depend on human ability. Such were my ideas the day God stopped me in my tracks in a most unusual way.

OOPS!

I walked into the pastor's office to turn down the job offer. He was in the midst of a phone conversation and invited me to sit in a big red leather chair until he finished. No sooner had I sat down than this horrible clammy sweat and nausea began to coat my body from my feet upward.

I prayed, "Lord, what is going on?" He replied, "You are making a mistake."

On the spot, I decided to stay in Granada Hills and serve the pastor and congregation. The sickness immediately subsided. When Pastor Miller got off the phone and asked what I came for, I smiled and replied I just wanted to reaffirm my commitment to the job.

APPRENTICESHIP

Those next three years were some of the best of my life. As an apprentice to Pastor Art, I matured and learned practical elements of the ministry. Yet, I nearly missed this wonderful opportunity for growth by my pride and impatience. Looking back on the school and my job, I had felt ready to take on the world. God stopped me, but he had to use momentary sickness to get my attention. I was still too much in control. My desire to start a church was healthy, even God-given. My timing was lousy and selfish. The church had made a large investment in me. Now I was ready to run away without giving them time to reap the harvest of their patience and labor. The Granada Hills years were fun. God taught me much through Art Miller. I made several costly mistakes, often angering people, but Art backed me up and piloted me through often treacherous waters.

The church was healing, healthy and growing. I was able to learn from the congregation's mistakes as well as successes. I also became convinced that classroom education can never substitute for on-the-job training under a skilled mentor. Art coached me, the kids I served shaped my thinking. Actually doing the ministry under the shelter of an established church built practicality into my thinking. The whole process was a divinely orchestrated birthing process for a pretty well incubated baby pastor.

Two kids in the Granada Hills youth group really stood out. Dan Boyd was a tall, lanky 12-year-old with braces when we met. By the time I was hired, he was 15 and a real clown. Jeff Miller was the pastor's son and I had known him since he was about eight. They were all good kids but Dan and Jeff stood out whenever concern for the Lord would show. Both Dan and Jeff became leaders in the youth group and today both are successful leaders in the Foursquare Movement. Dan is the pastor of Hope Chapel in Santa Rosa, California. Jeff works as an executive in one of our regional offices. Their buddies Bill Vega, Dan's brother Dudley, and Jeff's brother Rodney were a welcomed backdrop of uproarious jokes and pranks.

When my 15-year-old brother-in-law Tim Correa moved in with Ruby and me, it was Dan who first befriended him. And it was Jeff who found a job for him. When Tim accepted the Lord, Dan taught him to live like a Christian.

Under Dan and Jeff's leadership, many young people came to Christ and a very effective witness went out to the largest high school in the country. They organized a six a.m. prayer meeting every Tuesday morning with about 30 high schoolers in attendance. They held a Bible study at noon on the campus, singing Jesus songs right next to the radical "Students for a Democratic Society." A couple of SDS leaders were saved as a result.

After two or three years, I was feeling so secure that I didn't want to leave. I brushed aside ever pioneering a church. I read about a 76-year-old man in New York state who was a youth director in a very large church and ran a youth meeting with 900 kids every week. I decided that was for me. I was going to do what he did.

I had another day in the pastor's office. I walked in, and I made a big announcement: that I was going to commit the rest of my life to that job. I was going to stay there and minister until I retired. Even as I said the words, I had a sinking feeling inside me that God had other plans. The process of leaving Granada Hills really began before it all had started.

COVETING A BEACH TOWN

Early in my college days I had taken a bunch of junior high school boys from the church to Lunada Bay in Palos Verdes to go snorkeling. On the way home we were driving up Manhattan Beach Boulevard toward the freeway. As we were cruising along in my Volkswagen convertible, I thought "I'd love to live at the beach. I wonder if our denomination has a church in this town. If so, I want to pastor it." A really covetous, carnal thought. I was lusting for life in a beach town and for someone else's job.

About half a block later, by the fire station on Manhattan Beach Boulevard, there sat a tiny Foursquare church. As I looked at it, my first feeling was guilt, "Oh I shouldn't have been praying that way. That's really stupid. How carnal!"

After that day, whenever I remembered that church, I would pray that God would bless the community through that pastor. I prayed that way often, not knowing why.

I didn't know that a man named Carl Maclean had pastored that church faithfully for seven or eight years. He and his son, Jim, had built that building almost by themselves. Just about the time of my coveting session in the car, he died of a heart attack. More than likely, the building killed him.

Several years later, while living in Granada Hills, and feeling very secure in my job, I received a phone call from a friend of mine named Roy Hicks, Jr. He had just been offered a job as a pastor of a church in Eugene, Oregon. He called me and said, "I want you to come and help me. The church has a duplex. You can have half of it to live in. They pay $90 a week. I'll give you $40 of it to become assistant pastor."

I wanted to go. Roy was someone I deeply loved and respected, a real dear friend. I told him I would pray about it. I hung up and got on my knees, hoping that God would endorse the move. I hardly started to pray when I heard what *seemed* like an audible voice. It was as if someone was standing to my right, just behind me. The voice said, "What if Manhattan Beach opens up and you're in Oregon?" So I got right back on the phone. I told Roy, "I'm not coming, I don't think the Lord wants me there."

He laughed, "You sure prayed fast. It hasn't even been five minutes since I called you." I wasn't about to tell him I thought I heard God *talk* to me. I figured he'd think I was crazy. A few months later I shared the story with a friend of mine, Jim Hayford, Jack's brother. Jim was receptive and told me that he had experienced a similar sense of calling to a particular city.

JUST GO!

A year or so later, I went to lunch with Jim who was then the district youth director for Foursquare churches in Southern California. The day before we met, the district supervisor offered

Jim the church in Manhattan Beach. The congregation had called it quits and the plan was for Jim to turn it into a Christian coffee house. He refused. Now, he reminded me, "Hey, do you still want to go there? I remember what you told me a couple of years ago."

I replied sarcastically, "Yeah, I'll go there tomorrow." My wife had just quit her job to give birth to our son, and our family income had just dropped by 70 percent. We were struggling just to get by. Moving to the beach would mean having no salary at all—just living by faith. That didn't appeal to a certified "clinger to the ring" like me.

So, here we were sitting around at this restaurant making jokes about starting a church at the beach. "You could tow banners behind submarines with Scripture verses to witness to the skin divers, or you could hire an airplane to tow a 'Jesus Loves You' banner." We were having a smart-aleck's good time when I heard the voice again. No one else in the crowded restaurant turned around, so I knew it wasn't audible, but it seemed that way again.

Someone right behind me said, "Go!" The voice was stern and implied, "I don't like your jokes; they're not at all funny!"

I looked at Jim and said, "You know, maybe we should take this more seriously." I wasn't about to tell him I was hearing a voice. We decided I should go home and tell my wife Ruby. If she was in favor, we would move; if not, we'd stay put. When I got home, I was sure that she would say no. Our son Carl was six- months-old, we'd rented a house for the first time in five years of marriage, and I was discussing a job with no guarantee of income.

But she went for it. The next day we approached the district supervisor, Dr. Nathaniel Van Cleave. He had previously been my pastor and professor so he took a strong personal interest in our well-being. He tried to talk us out of going, saying, "I want to send you some place where there is an existing congregation. I don't want to send you into hardship." I finally had to tell him about the Lord talking to me. His response was, "Oh, so it's that way. Then go, by all means, go!" He recognized the voice of God while I felt so fearful of it.

4

GOING, GOING, GONE!

The move to Manhattan Beach severely loosened my grip on that old ring. The project was bigger than anything in my past. The consequences of failure would now affect my wife and infant son as well as myself. I had long before surrendered my life to the Lord. What I couldn't surrender were the details. I would follow willingly, if I could spell out the circumstances. Control takes many forms. In this case it appeared as fear.

When we want control, we are coveting God's position in our life. This is the root of sin. Lucifer tried to take God's position and was thrown out of heaven. Adam and Eve ate the forbidden fruit because it promised the power of choice and would make them *like God*. They were thrown out of the Garden of Eden. We grasp for control and want to usurp God's role in our lives. When we do, we are thrown out of his will and his promise of blessing. God doesn't want us to be robots. He does want alert, but trusting people who will obey even in the face of risk. The eleventh chapter of Hebrews details the lives of the faithful, the risk takers, those men and women who consistently surrendered their plans to the Lord.

God expects the same of us. And my move to the beach demanded surrender.

TAKING THE PLUNGE

We were guaranteed the use of the Manhattan Beach building plus $150 per month to help with overhead. I could take up to 60 percent of the offering per week. But where there were no people, there would be no offerings. The church building, by that time, had been closed for more than four months. We were church-planting in an empty building.

My wife, our baby son and myself, along with my brother-in-law and his friend, moved into an apartment in a run-down section of Redondo Beach in August 1971. Our rent was $225 a month. Our life savings was $2,100. We started church services in mid-September that year.

SOMETHING NEW . . .

During my years at Granada Hills, a man named Leland Davis was acclaimed a prophet by everyone who knew him. I wasn't so sure. A kind of traveling evangelist, he made the rounds to our church in Granada Hills about once a year. He would interrupt his preaching to prophesy to individuals in the church about very personal things in their lives.

I was troubled by it all. I thought he was a hoax, but couldn't say so because his sister, Ella, was a dear friend of my wife and mine. Then he prophesied to my friend Ray Boyd, concerning God's blessing in his many business ventures. Every bit of it came true. Suddenly, Leland Davis had my attention.

At a later date, he spoke *to me* in front of the entire congregation. I was first embarrassed, then frightened as he detailed how I was to fall out of favor with the church and then be restored to a place of respect and fruitful ministry. I'll spare you the details, but that prophesy was fulfilled with painful reality, followed by wonderful blessing.

Two weeks before our departure to the beach, Leland came back to Granada Hills. He had another message from the Lord: "The Lord wants you to know that he is going to do a new work through you and through a church that doesn't yet exist. You are to trust him and move with the Spirit. It will be different from anything you have seen or can anticipate. It is going to be a brand-new thing, you are to relax and trust him to do it." Two months later, in another situation, with no possible knowledge of Leland's words, a lady said almost the same thing. She addressed her words to the whole group, but I felt God was telling me to trust him and not lean on my own devices.

More than a year later on the first anniversary of "Hope Chapel," we had a guest speaker named Ray Mossholder. After the service, several of us were standing around talking in the back of the auditorium.

Ray suddenly said, "Let's pray." We did until he interrupted with a "word from the Lord." It was as if he quoted the words of Leland and that woman—with one difference. He said, "You can't even pray for this, the Lord is going to do something brand new and you can't even visualize it to pray for it." Again, God was saying, "Don't try so hard to control things." He wants us to learn that he knows what he is doing, even when we don't have all the details. When we relax and trust, we become flexible and more responsive to our calling.

LET GO AND LET GOD!

I saw the words "Let Go and Let God!" on a bumper sticker last week. It is a clever, oversimplified way to summarize everything I'm trying to say in this book. Ours was to be a walk by faith, not by sight. God is as interested in the process toward reaching the goal as he is in the accomplishment at its destination. He wants us to let go, but that is seldom enough. He wants us to mature, too.

Growth always involves pain. It usually works like this: We let go. Then we encounter difficulties and freak out. We turn to God, tremble awhile, and finally are rescued by a work of the Spirit. Paul tells us to rejoice about the process. He writes, "We can rejoice, too, when we run into problems and trials, for we know that they are good for us--they help us learn to endure" (Romans 5:3 NLT). Paul further states that endurance generates strength of character which raises expectations of victory. Victory is assured because of the love of God which will never disappoint us (Romans 5:4-5). However you state it, there *is* a price to be paid and a race to be run. But, the guarantee of success is his continuous love and support. Because of him, we win in the end.

Consider a 25-year-old preacher with no guaranteed income, in a car with more than 154,000 miles on its odometer, driving his wife and infant son around in the heat of August, looking for shelter in the midst of a housing shortage. Add to that a three-piece suit and a whitewall haircut in a day when everyone was into long hair and ragged clothes. Place the guy in a church building designed for 72 persons with a parking lot built for just seven cars. Put a vision in his heart for 2,000 people and stand him, suit and all, behind a monstrous pulpit trying to preach to 20 people, including several bikers, a marine corporal, a tiny baby and a topless dancer.

You have a picture of a guy with plenty of trouble to rejoice over. You also have a description of me on my third Sunday as pastor of Hope Chapel.

UP AND (BARELY) RUNNING

The first week was relatively easy. Only 12 people in the church, all friends. We just sat in a circle and had Bible study.

A friend from Granada Hills named Ron Parks was in the Marine Corps stationed at Camp Pendleton. He brought his mother to play the piano, his sister Susie and her boyfriend Mickie. A young girl from Granada Hills, Diane Bennett, showed up as did Wally and Joyce Larson, who would drive 180 miles a Sunday for three months just to help us get started. My own household accounted for the rest, including my young brother-in-law, Tim Correa and my six-month-old son, Carl. By this time, a friend named Spencer Morris moved in with our family and joined the leadership team.

By the third week, I was desperate. The nature of our congregation changed radically in one day. Susie Parks had brought a friend, Toni Corbett, on the second Sunday. We led her to the Lord two days later. Toni proved to be an evangelist, bringing her mother, two sisters, their boyfriends and about 10 other people. Among them were some pretty rough people that

I didn't know how to handle. That third week I went home and cried, "Lord, what am I doing here? I'm not cut out to pastor these people. I'm out of control."

My crisis was triggered when one of Toni's friends, Mike Howard, tried to open a sticky door. I went over to help him. Picture this in your mind: me with my three-piece suit and short hair trying to help this big biker clad in a black leather jacket, engineer boots with steel bottoms and flaming red hair past his shoulders. The door wouldn't open no matter how we shoved. Mike got angry, stepped back, and kicked the door open, while yelling at the top of his voice. The door broke. I was scared, really scared.

I thought I didn't fit and could never adequately pastor Mike and his friends. I just wanted to run away from the whole project.

BACKBONE OF THE CHURCH

The real problem was my control-oriented, stereotyped view of the ministry. When I finally relaxed, those "rough looking, long-hairs" turned out to be the backbone of the church. Incidentally, Mike is now a graduate of LIFE Bible College and has worked on our pastoral staff. His friend and fellow ex-drug abuser, Randy Weir, engaged himself in ministry by picking up hitchhikers on Pacific Coast Highway so he could tell them about Jesus. Randy went on to help plant three churches including Hope Chapel Ventura where he is the founding pastor. Nearly three decades later, his son is on staff with my son in a youth ministry in Huntington Beach. Another of those early converts, John Hille, married a wonderful woman named

Charlotte Bohot. They soon planted a church in Houston, Texas. "Let go and let God" is not easy, but it sure works.

In spite of all the dramatic stories of the early years, I dare not forget one wonderful, if quiet person. Her name was Mary Deriberprey. This soft-spoken Puerto Rican lady was already retired when we started the church. Yet she remained active in our ministry until she passed away at eighty-something years of age in 1997. She was, in fact, our first member. The final few weeks before the church was padlocked, there had been just Mary along with the former pastor and his wife.

The building had been closed for several months and we had reopened it for about two months before she discovered us. Mary became one of the pillars of our church. Her age and stability demonstrated that Christianity worked in the long term. In those days, she didn't yet speak a lot of English, but was very fluent in "love," the language of God's kingdom. She brought hope to our young adults. It was Mary, by her actions, who taught me that Hope Chapel really only exists for "young" people. This includes the *physically* young and those *grey-haired* young folks who are so flexible because they exude the love of Jesus. Mary set an example to the young because of her longevity in Christ. She was a perfect example to older people of someone fulfilling her assignment to train the young in wisdom, family and submission to God in every area of life (Titus 2:4-5). After we moved to Hawaii, her letters were a monthly source of strength and encouragement to me. And I also know her prayers stood strong in the face of satanic opposition to our new church. Mary is a real treasure and one of the first people I'll look for when I get to heaven.

OUR ANCHOR OF HOPE

The name "Hope Chapel" didn't come easily. My wife and I tossed names around for weeks. We bored our friends with a continual flow of church names. It finally came to three choices.

Had we thought to check our phone book, we could have saved ourselves a lot of wasted energy. As it was, late one night we drove around South Bay only to discover our top three choices for church names firmly attached to existing church buildings. Very depressing!

Our opening date pressed hard upon us. The first service in the "First-Church-of-No-Name-in-the-Little-Green-Building-on-Manhattan-Beach-Boulevard" didn't seem real exciting. It was time to lay aside the brainstorms in favor of prayer.

Not to say we didn't pray before. But now we let go of the situation and simply committed it to the Lord. He came through in one stroke.

It happened while I was out visiting high school students from the church in Granada Hills. I felt the Spirit tugging in a new direction. Exiting a home in Reseda, my next stop was in the Santa Clarita Valley, 20 miles to the north. As I drove to the freeway, my brain kept getting signals to drive to the Valley Book and Bible Store in Van Nuys. The store was south of me and several miles out of my way.

The impressions only grew stronger as I continued the drive into the Santa Clarita Valley. Upon arriving, I gave in and U-turned to Van Nuys. (No, I didn't quickly finish my business in the Santa Clarita Valley. If you let go of the ring, you've got to let go completely.)

By the time I got to the store, I was convinced the Lord sent me so he could give me a name for our church.

I felt a little foolish, but I was determined I would walk in the front door, through the aisles, all the way to the back. If something caught my eye, I would investigate. If not, I would go back to the Santa Clarita Valley.

The first thing I noticed was a plaque with a crude anchor accompanied by the word "hope." The same symbol appeared on bookends, jewelry, etc. My cynical heart told me that fish and crosses had reached market saturation, so maybe anchors were good for a few more bucks.

I walked to the back of the store and nothing seemed especially noteworthy. I did, however, notice a new book by Francis Schaeffer. As I reached for it, I saw another book describing early Christian symbolism, and thought, "Maybe God sent me here to get a church name out of this book." Sure enough, there was that anchor with a detailed explanation of its significance.

During the second century of Roman persecution, no one wore crosses on their lapels or Christian bumper stickers on their chariots. Faith in Jesus Christ was only secretly revealed to a trusted friend or neighbor.

One method of revelation was for a person to secretly draw an anchor that looked like our capital letter *J* backwards. If his acquaintance were uninitiated, he would seem to be simply doodling. But, if the other person were a Christian, they would align another, normal *J* symbol to the doodle so that it became an anchor. The anchor was a symbol for Christ, who is the anchor of our souls.

The whole concept is paraphrased by Hebrews 6:19 (KJV): "This hope we have as an anchor of the soul, a hope both sure and steadfast. . . ."

Early Mediterranean sailors had a trick for overcoming windless days on the ocean. They would load the ship's anchor into a smaller boat and row a few kilometers in the direction of travel. When the line was fully extended, they dropped anchor. At that time, their peers on the ship would winch in the anchor rope, pulling the vessel forward. It was laborious, but it worked. The smaller boat was called the *forerunner*, but it was the anchor that offered a way of travel— Jesus is our hope; he is our anchor.

We picked up the anchor symbol for our logo and called the congregation "Hope Chapel." Our hope being Jesus himself, who has gone before us as a forerunner and an anchor to assure our arrival in a place he has prepared for us.

Though it was a Biblical name, we took a lot of flack for it. It seems other pastors dealt in faith, which they saw as more valid than hope. In ignorance, they threw away an important scriptural concept.

The Lord, though, understands hope and hopeless people. He gave us a name that offers a promise of help and a new way of life. Hope is as necessary to the president of a thriving company as it is to the homeless person in the street. Everyone is looking for an anchor.

OLD FEARS

As Hope Chapel Manhattan Beach got going, I reencountered an old hang-up. It was my fear about my own leadership potential. I had enjoyed some pretty exciting times in the ministry in Granada Hills. On a couple of occasions, we had twice as many people at a youth activity as we had in the whole congregation. But for some reason, the youth group only measured about 30 kids who attended consistently. This was only one-tenth of the draw to our major events. As a result, I had this misconception that I was only capable of pastoring about 30 people. This fear cost me many nights of sleep.

When we started the church, we had fewer than 30 people for several weeks. There would be 22 people or 24, or 28, then 21 people again—but never more than 30. I was really frustrated and sought the Lord for a breakthrough. Those prophecies about God doing a new thing became terribly important. Fear was a blessing, because it drove me to seek the Lord. I gained a deeper understanding of God and of my role as a pastor.

MENTORS AT A DISTANCE

God indeed did a new work, but it came in some unexpected ways. His answers came through the encouragement and example of two very dissimilar people, Robert Schuller and Chuck Smith. Ruby and I heard Schuller teach a seminar at the Crystal Cathedral in Garden Grove. We were impressed with his faith. I had already read his book *Move Ahead with Possibility Thinking*. In the book, he told of his own fears and frustration in early pastoral ministry. He also outlined his intent to seek the Lord, and grow in faith, which he calls "possibility thinking." Over and over in that seminar I heard the statement, "With men this is impossible; but with God all things are possible" (Matthew 19:26 KJV). He also said, "If there is something you think

God has called you to do and if there is any way you can envision accomplishing it, then it probably wasn't God calling. Because God will only call you to do things that are bigger than you are, something bigger than your personal resources."

He spoke right into my frustration. I thought that I couldn't be pastor to more than about 30 people. Yet, I felt that God was showing me that the church would grow to more than 2,000 people (the actual number he put into my head was 2,200). I even believed that God had directed me to a building which would house a congregation of that size. Both the congregation size and the building cost were impossibilities of the first rank. Schuller's words rang in my ears as a bid to greater faith.

Dr. Schuller told how he had found himself stuck off out to the side of a highway as he was driving to California to start Crystal Cathedral. He had $500 in his pocket and an organ on a little trailer. He had gotten a good start and was halfway across the country when a rear tire on his car went flat. He pulled off the side of the road only to discover that his tire jack didn't work. There was no way to change the tire. Faced with this problem, he began to pray, asking God what to do. The Lord directed him to dig a hole underneath the tire with the tire iron. He dug deep enough to get the old tire off and put the new one on. It was a great illustration on how the Lord will show us a way to get through any obstacle that stands in the way of ministry.

The primary message of the conference was to "find a need and fill it." This meant looking for hurting people and praying for grace and wisdom to minister to them. When you address suffering, you're often forced to find solutions that don't yet exist. But the Lord is creative and, if you seek him, he gives innovative wisdom. He also deals in miraculous answers to prayer. Schuller taught me to walk the unpaved road.

Find a Need and Fill It

A bit of homework, necessary to the seminar, involved listing the 10 greatest unmet needs in our community. We found several obvious problems in our town. One was locked up in the narcotic revolution. Everyone under 30 seemed to be experimenting with drugs. The churches were upset, but not reaching out. Most Christian leaders condemned the drug users without offering any spiritual solutions to their dilemma. In those days if you didn't dress like everyone else, you weren't welcome in church. People using drugs weren't putting on white shirts and ties to come to church. We were different. We cared, but had few resources. If we bought into this area of service, God would have to provide for us.

Another need in our community was for a church that could minister to single adults. If you weren't in high school or college and you weren't married, the church didn't know what to do with you. It was worse if you were divorced. If you were a single parent, for whatever-the-reason, you could forget the church. No other church wanted to deal with singles, so we chose to get involved. We decided to cut as narrow a slice of the sociological pie as we could and do the best job possible with these people. Finding a need, we set out to fill it. We ran ads in the paper and distributed literature targeted at young single adults, particularly those who had been associated with the drug culture.

You can imagine what happened. Many churches in the South Bay reacted against us. We were "just a hippie church," and I was a "young punk who wasn't interested in meeting the needs of whole families."

I was involved with families; I wanted to help create them. I prayed that God would turn our church into a "mating ground" for young Christian adults. Too often, I had watched young Christians become discouraged looking for a mate. They'd finally wander into a bar looking for love. Then their life would go down the drain. One or two kids and a load of debt later, they would wander back into church looking for help. I wanted to break the cycle.

I prayed that God would send single adults into our fellowship. We hoped that he would introduce them to each other and that we could perform lots of Christian marriages. Hope Chapel was built on the answer to that prayer and builds strong families as a result. The same prayer holds for Hope Chapel Kaneohe. We intend to pass the gospel on to the next generation. We realize that involves the formulation of new families by remaining attractive to single adults. It is a major priority.

A Very Warm Smile

Just before starting the church, Ruby and I attended a Foursquare pastor's conference. It was there that we heard a speaker who overwhelmed us with his testimony. I could easily identify with this man and a life long respect for him was born in my heart that evening. He, too, was ministering to young single adults. A lot of them were hippies that had flocked into Orange County in those days. No counterculture icon, here was a middle-aged man with a bald head and gray hair. He wore a tan business suit supported by a black turtleneck sweater. Before speaking, he paused and smiled for what seemed like minutes.

That smile was about half a mile wide. I'd never seen such warmth in my entire life.

Of course this was Chuck Smith, pastor of Calvary Chapel in Costa Mesa, California. He told how God had earlier released him from the ministry. During that time he had shed any taste for tradition and gimmickry in the church. Later the Lord brought him back into the pulpit by way of a home Bible study. Later he accepted the call to pastor a small congregation in the Newport Beach area.

He was intrigued by all the young people turning to drugs and wanted to meet a hippie. Chuck told how his son invited a young longhair home to meet his dad, the pastor. This young man lived on Pacific Coast Highway, hitchhiking back and forth between Canada and Mexico. His goal was to declare the gospel to whoever gave him a ride. Greatly impressed, Chuck hired him as youth pastor. The church supplied their new staff member with a two-bedroom house. Within a couple of weeks there were 40 people living in that tiny house and yard. With this event, God exploded Calvary Chapel into significance. A youth movement was born that would result in several hundred thousand people finding Jesus Christ in just a few years. The total result stretches into the millions as Calvary changed the face and posture of church in America and throughout much of the world.

Untraditional Ministry

That night, I knew God had sent me to receive basic instruction from this man. He taught us to cope with growth by shifting around the church program. I was used to the traditional church, with a full-scale Sunday school meeting early on

Sundays, followed by a traditional worship service. That type of program demands facilities and a big management team. We had neither. Our church was built to house 72 people. We only had 30, but we were looking toward 2,000.

Chuck said that they had done away with adult Sunday school. He just taught the Bible to adults in church while the kids enjoyed Sunday school. The whole ministry was aimed at Bible education. This model allowed us to move into multiple services. We could stretch the logistical capabilities of our small building. That met our need for space.

Chuck pressed the issue of actually *teaching* Scripture rather than just entertaining or comforting God's people. He restored the role of prophet and teacher to the church. He even addressed church growth from a different angle. He challenged us through Jesus' statements to Peter: (A) Jesus told Peter that *he*, not Peter, would be responsible for building his church (Matthew 16:18). (B) He informed Peter that his role was that of a shepherd, feeding his sheep (John 21:15-17). In other words, a pastor should equip the saints and leave church growth up to the Lord. Jesus would bring growth through new birth as the Christians grew to maturity.

I'd spent my whole life trying to figure out how to build a church. I attended annual seminars looking for *the* new plan. It took years for me to discover the reason for the grand new plans was that the old ones never worked.

Here, Chuck Smith was quoting Jesus, and Jesus wasn't telling Peter (or me) to build a church. He was saying that *Jesus* would build *his* church. That turned me on. Chuck also reminded us that Jesus told Peter it was his job to feed the sheep.

Most pastors I knew put "sheep feeding" very low on their priority list. I was one of them. This is a formula for spiritual disaster as recorded by the Old Testament chronicler of Israel. He wrote eloquently about how lousy things went in Judah without a *teaching prophet* (2 Chronicles 15:3-6). Too often the church lacks a teaching prophet and the people are like starving sheep. Chuck said his mandate as a pastor was to tend the lambs and feed the sheep, and that meant to serve God's Word in generous helpings. It was Jesus' job to build his church.

At that time, Calvary Chapel was the fastest growing, and soon to be the largest, church in North America.

Chuck didn't have any secrets, other than doing what the Lord had said, and anyone could obey the Lord if he chose. Through his example, I discovered my primary assignment: "Teach the Bible, very well!"

Robert Schuller said, "Find a need," and pointed me toward single adults. Chuck Smith said, "Feed the flock." He role modeled Bible teaching, verse-by-verse, defining words and teaching historical context. God gave us a workable game plan through those two men. With it, we couldn't help but be successful.

WONDERFULLY "BUMMED OUT"!

The church soon began to grow. My teaching slowly improved. Young and old attended our services and love mostly abounded in our midst. But, life was not free from discouragement. I remember one middle-aged couple who came during the first four months in Manhattan Beach. They took us out to dinner a couple of times. Even brought flowers to my wife. We embraced them as friends and mentors. Then, one day the woman called to tearfully inform me that she wasn't coming to church anymore. The teaching was shallow. It just didn't meet her needs. Black despair filled my heart and mind as I hung up the phone. Our attendance may have grown past 30, but I was hurting that my teaching wasn't up to par.

While I prayed and agonized before the Lord, the same lady called back and took me off the hook. Now she was angry. "Well, I just had to tell you one more thing about the church, and maybe this is the real reason we're not going there. Would those people dress that way if Jesus came to that church?" *Click!*

I realized that this lady wasn't going to have her needs met anywhere. She focused on outward appearances, not new hearts. Jesus *was* coming to our church and he *was* saving "long-hairs" who came to the church barefoot and dirty. He was radically changing hopeless, wrecked lives through the teaching of the Scriptures. That poor woman was trapped by religious tradition and a particular style of dress. She couldn't see the miracles because she wouldn't look past the clothing into people's eyes. Later, I came under other pressures to be a little more "middle-of-the-road" and especially to lay off the singles focus. The old ring made an occasional surprise appearance when the pressure came from our biggest contributors. But that first woman became a catalyst. In the beginning, I pastored whoever came. As a result of her phone call(s), I chose to pastor hurting people. As Jesus said, "It is the sick who need a physician" (Mark 2:17).

REACHING OUT

Any new church must find identity in its leadership and in the style of outreach. In many ways, the latter will affect the former. Early success in evangelism and outreach colors the leadership and their view of the world. This was certainly true in our case.

THE CROSS AND THE SWITCHBLADE

In our first year, we gave away 20,000 copies of David Wilkerson's book *The Cross and the Switchblade* in an attempt to let people know that God cared about them. Wilkerson was an Assembly of God pastor in a small Pennsylvania mountain town. God called him to New York to witness to five young men on trial for beating a quadriplegic to death in his wheelchair. Unable to contact the men, Wilkerson charged into the courtroom. Hurled out by the bailiff, his picture made the front page of the *New York Times*. He never did see the young men he had gone to visit, but the kids in the ghettos saw him as a hero. A prominent gang leader was born again shortly after threatening to kill Wilkerson. Their relationship gave birth to a ministry called Teen Challenge. This group is hugely successful at helping people off drugs and out of gangs through the power of the Holy Spirit.

We didn't have a gang problem, but drugs were everywhere. The book would be a perfect giveaway for our location. I contacted a Christian philanthropist named W. Clement Stone, who had given Wilkerson money to start Teen Challenge. Stone was also a friend of Robert Schuller. We knew where we could purchase *The Cross and the Switchblade* books for 25 cents each, so we wrote Mr. Stone asking for $5,000 to buy 20,000 copies. There were only 20 of us in the church at the time when I wrote the letter. That meant distributing 1,000 books each. Mr. Stone gave us the money. We bought the books and attached a little red sticker that read, "Need help? Call Hope Chapel," offering my home telephone number as a 24-hour hot line.

By the time the books arrived, we were six months into the church. There were now 100 of us. That meant we only had to give away 200 books apiece. Still 20,000 copies of a small paperback book will fill a large semi-trailer truck almost to capacity. Eight people worked a whole day just attaching the labels.

Although we'd been given the books, which could retail for $20,000, we did have to buy the labels which cost $72. Our finances were so tight that I wrote a hot check on Friday afternoon to pay for the stickers. All day Saturday, I fervently prayed that Sunday's offering would cover it. It did, but only because the offering was extraordinarily large that day.

In three weeks, the books were gone. Those 21 days were some of the most exciting in the history of our church. Churches often come asking their neighbors for help. This church came offering to help the community. When we handed someone a paperback book, he thought we'd given him a dollar (1972 price of a paperback book). It was nice. Individuals who wouldn't talk about the Lord took time to read the book. We gave them to people everywhere. A group of us smothered a mile of beach on a Saturday afternoon, giving books to everyone we met. I'd even stand outside a couple of nearby junior high schools at three o'clock giving the books to students on their way home.

Incidentally, one day when I was telling this story 12 years later, a very lovely young woman walked up to me. She was new to our church and said, "You know, I remember you coming to my junior high in Manhattan Beach and giving away those books. I visited the church a few times, but I've just now become a Christian. I came here to join because of those books."

We went to hospitals because we knew that patients had extra reading time. Of course, we also gave them to our friends and family.

A young longhair named John Hille walked into Hawthorne City Jail with a box of books asking, "Who's in charge of drugs here?" The sergeant bolted out of his chair like he thought the box was full of marijuana. John explained that he wanted to distribute books telling how God could change drug abusers and gang members. The guy replied, "I've got the keys to the jail. Let's go." The two of them gave away a case of books in 15 minutes.

The plan worked. People came to the Lord. We counseled hundreds of people over the phone and many times the Lord delivered people on hard drugs in an instant when they'd been unsuccessful in long-term drug programs. The neat thing was that we cast ourselves in a servant's role that would result in long-lasting ministry.

One funny little sideline to all this came in the form of people who'd use the hot line number to play pranks on me. Countless Saturday nights were marked by someone calling up to be silly with the sound of a party in the background. Pranks are to be expected, but I sure lost a lot of sleep. But, the hassles were worth enduring, especially when some of the pranksters accepted the Lord and joined our fellowship.

WAVES OF FAITH

Finances were very tight during the first six months. My salary one awful week came to $15. By comparison, the minimum wage was more than $100 for the same period.

Finances got tighter when my wife discovered that we were about to become parents of a beautiful baby girl. God had used the birth of our son, Carl, to put us in a tight spot, and he used the arrival of Kelly to keep us there. Financial limitations drove us to greater faith and more inventive outreach.

We had very little to spend on advertising, so we created a literature piece called "Waves of Faith." It was a bright green, legal-sized page printed on both sides with testimonies of people in Hope Chapel. Best of all, it cost only about $24 per thousand pieces. Then I would put on my tennis shoes and run through the neighborhood leaving literature on every door. I could hit 125 houses an hour for a four-hour stretch. I lost a little weight, but hand delivery was cheaper than paying postage.

For every thousand pieces I put out, a family would join our church. It paid off. Even now, I'm still in contact with most of the people who came directly or indirectly through that effort. Among them—David Benefiel, Barry Felis, Randy Boldt, Steven Steffe, Greg Frazier, Dale Yancy, and Bobby Chance, all went on to pastoral ministry. Dale has personally planted three congregations and can boast of a bunch of daughter and granddaughter churches.

Because I moved quickly, I seldom spoke with any of the residents. But one day as I was fastening a brochure to her door, the lady of the house opened it. I handed her the literature, and she said, "Oh, my daughter might be interested in this." Her daughter, Sue, was dating the leader of a Christian rock band called "Children of the Light." I'd been hoping to hire the group to play at our church, but I didn't know how to contact them. As a result with my encounter with her mother, Sue came to Hope. She brought her boyfriend, Randy Boldt, and his partners. Later, I was still struggling to contact the band when someone said, "They all go to your church." Meanwhile, the guys were all wondering why we hadn't asked them to play.

OF COACHES AND PLAYERS

Two thousand houses a week was a nice literature goal, but it couldn't last forever. I couldn't remain responsible for bringing new people through the front door. A pastor needs help in order to fulfill his calling. The Bible teaches pastors and other leaders to build up or equip everyone else to do the work of the ministry (Ephesians 4:11-13). The pastor who does all the work may have lots of control, but the church will remain stunted. The church works like a football team. Players, not coaches, win games on the field. The coaches exist to train and equip players. This became our strategy for expanded ministry.

Pop gospel singer Andrae Crouch gave us an opportunity to test this new strategy. I had gone to college with Andrae, but barely knew him. He was only in the school for two years before his ministry flourished and he left. Several years later, a mutual friend invited me to one of Andrae's huge concerts in Orange County. I sat there feeling sorry for myself. I was pastor of such a small church (only three-months-old) and we could never afford to host someone like Andrae. I griped to the Lord throughout the whole evening. Late that night, my friend called. He had scheduled a dinner meeting with Andrae to discuss a big South Bay outreach. He wondered, "Is it all right to bring Andrae to sing in church after the dinner?"

We *only* told the people in our church. We didn't go on the radio or in the newspaper. I didn't even go house-to-house with fliers. This was a special opportunity for our people to invite friends. There were about 40 people in the church, and we said they could invite *only* their friends. We had equipped our members. Now we handed them the ball. One hundred twenty-five people showed up. The building was crowded to overflowing. People sat outside, enjoying the music and message through the windows. God taught us to use an event, our literature, or whatever else to support our members in *their* outreach ministry. This strategy caused many of those young Christians to embrace responsibility and leadership. We believe this strategy is the major force behind our ultimate success at planting churches.

"AVON CALLING"

During those early months, my wife sold Avon cosmetic products to keep us in groceries. She managed to get the route that included the immediate neighborhood of our church building. Her route included about 200 homes and apartments. Every time we created a new literature piece, we left it attached to those particular screen doors. People became aware of the church through the literature. They grew as interested in my wife and her testimony as in the products she sold. Several of those folks eventually found their way into our fellowship.

We stopped trying to use the literature to bring people to the Lord. Rather, we began to see it as a plow breaking the soil so our members could sow seeds of the gospel, face to face.

LOVE FEASTS

The idea of reinforcing the members in ministry produced a new tradition in Hope Chapel. Our first Thanksgiving we noticed that many of our people were living far away from their families. Several had left homes in the North or East to live the "good life" in California. Others had lived on the road and in very strange locations before they became Christians. During the early '70s a lot of people lived in parks or under the Manhattan Beach Pier. Many of these folks came to the Lord through our members. We couldn't leave them alone or in the cold for Thanksgiving, so we turned the auditorium and overflow room into a big dining hall.

One pew sat up against a folding wall, about 10 feet behind the next one leaving an aisle space in between. We set a ping-pong table in the aisle. Some sat on the pew and others sat in chairs on three sides of the table. Card tables went into the youth room, and our small office provided a serving area. We had our "After Thanksgiving Potluck Dinner" on Sunday night. This gave us the benefit of the leftovers from the actual holiday. It also allowed a special time for our church to become an extended family. Those who had much were able to share with those who possessed little. Later we discovered this was the exact motivation of the "Lord's Supper" practiced in the early church (1 Corinthians 11:20-21). We called our dinners Love Feasts after the "feasts of charity" mentioned later in the New Testament (Jude 1:12). We moved beyond Thanksgiving to schedule them several times a year.

Years later, we still construct buildings with small kitchens so we cannot host banquets. If our church is to eat together, it has to be a potluck.

THE SONSHINE INN

Another lesson in equipping our members to do God's work was called the "Sonshine Inn." A few young people asked if they could start a Christian coffee house in the space we used for that first Thanksgiving dinner. Now don't think Starbucks, here!

Those were the days of long hair and revolutions. Coffee houses were a cross between a nonalcoholic nightclub and the espresso houses where poets would spout their stuff in the days of the "beatniks." Christians used coffee houses to great advantage. They would often open up an old house as a place where 40 or 50 young people could sit on the floor and listen to music. These places fostered much evangelism. Although they were called coffee houses, very little coffee was served. This crowd was into soft drinks.

We couldn't afford to rent a house so we screened off the overflow room at the rear of our auditorium. Our young leaders went nuts. They put posters all over the walls and glued carpet scraps together in a patchwork floor cover. They put together a rock band of four or five regulars with musical instruments and called their creation "The Sonshine Inn."

We thought it would involve 10 or 15 young people every Saturday night. But they sometimes drew a bigger crowd on Saturdays than we did for Sunday morning church.

Through this vehicle, God taught us several things about ministry. First, we discovered that good things would happen if we simply got out of the way. This meant trusting potential leaders who were very young in the Lord. Too many pastors and elders hang onto that old ring at this point. When we retain close control, we hamper the Holy Spirit in the lives of others. We had let half a dozen new Christians run with the ball and substantial ministry resulted. The results were truly wonderful.

Second, the Sonshine Inn was a focal point for evangelism by young Christians. A person might share Christ well, but not have the courage to invite his friend to pray and ask the Lord into his life. The coffee house supplemented this process and became a harvest center. It was important that non-saved persons come by invitation rather than by advertisement, as the Sonshine Inn was only designed to complement ministry, not perform it.

Third, some people were regulars on Saturday but never showed up on Sunday due to job schedules. This taught us to provide multiple services to further serve our people.

Another nice lesson was that people, not properties, make a church. Every Sunday we lived with an auditorium that looked like a church in the front and a garage in the rear. Some people were a little uptight about all the mess. Their comments forced us to set priorities, and people won over facilities.

"FOAM RIDER"

Every society has its folk heroes. Hope Chapel is no different. I like to tell the story of Rick Fulenwider, or "Foam Rider" to all his surfing friends. This man epitomized the first four years of Hope Chapel.

It all started with Mike Howard (the biker who kicked the door open on our third Sunday). Mike began asking for prayer in every service. "Pray that I find my friend Rick. I think he's in jail, and I want to tell him about the Lord."

Pretty soon it became, "Praise the Lord, I found Rick! He just got out of jail for dealing. Pray that I can share the gospel with him." Then, "Pray for Rick. He nearly beat me up for nagging at him about the Lord."

One Wednesday night a couple of us were standing outside the building, teasing a guy named John about his haircut—he had whacked off his shoulder length-hair and shaved his beard. What a shock!

In the midst of this, two bikes came roaring up. Mike was one of them. The other guy we didn't know. He had hair down his back and a "Fu Manchu" moustache. He wore motorcycle boots and a denim jacket spotted with bleach. He drove a chopped Harley with flames painted all over the fenders and gas tank.

They parked the bikes and sauntered inside. As they passed us, Mike said, "Hi, you guys, this is Rick."

To get inside the building they had to pass Will Heinle. Will was an engineer at McDonnell-Douglas Corporation and served bivocationally as our first associate pastor. He was 58-years-old, bald on top with a closely-cropped fringe of white hair all around and wore a Polyester sports coat and tie. Hardly a close match for two bikers.

Will had a signature habit of introduction. He would say, "Hiya man," while grabbing your hand as if to shake it. He would then embrace you in a bear hug. Love oozed from the man. He caught Rick at the door on the way in.

The meeting was small—six or eight people. We were sharing testimonies when Rick spoke up: "I want to share something. Right here, right now I accepted Jesus Christ into my heart like Mike's been telling me. I've been mad at Mike for bugging me about the Lord and I came here tonight to beat up the pastor so Mike would get off my back, but . . ." he now pointed at Will, "that old man over there (sob, sob), he (sob, sob) hugged me. . . ." God's love didn't seem to know any "generation gap."

Rick Fulenwider helped me move into our new house the next weekend. My neighbors told me they were scared that he was moving in, not me. They could only see his hair and clothing. But God was at work, in the hidden corners of Rick's heart.

The man was still rough. One day we went surfing in Venice. Yes, Rick was a biker who was also a contest surfer with trophies to prove it. He was well known and much feared. Groups of people would stop talking when Rick approached. They showed him a sickening kind of respect.

One fairly tough-looking man told us he was going to steal some trunks out of the bag laying by the strand wall. Rick said, "God doesn't want you to do that."

The guy shot back, "God doesn't want me to steal? What about the guy whose head you busted when he caught you stealing his surfboard?"

Rick: "I said, God doesn't want you to steal those trunks."

The guy: "So what? Did you get religion or something?"

Rick (jaw tightening): "No, I'm a Christian and God doesn't want you to take those trunks."

The guy: "Oh, you're a Jesus freak!"

Rick was hot by now, and he grabbed the guy and repeated, "No, I'm a Christian . . ." The guy backed down.

Rick remained tough, but he was breaking. One day he came to church crying with remorse. He had punched some guy while they were surfing and then tried to apologize and share the gospel with him. The other surfer accepted the apology, but passed on the preaching. His rejection devastated Rick.

He used to "prophesy" in church. Just before I'd preach he'd stand up with a real imposing voice and tell everyone, "That little skinny guy in the suit is our preacher and God talks through him, so you better listen—especially you new people." You can imagine how his behavior created a "seeker sensitive" environment for our church.

Over time, God smoothed the rough edges off a man who loved him with his whole heart. One day Rick wept as he told me how he wanted to marry a godly woman. We began to agree in prayer that God would provide him with a Christian wife.

Another time he testified how five men in an old car intentionally knocked him and a friend off his bike, with their car, at a red light. He pulled the lock chain off the motorcycle and went after them. "I was going to cut the leader's head in two until the Holy Spirit stopped me. . . ." Rick told the man to wait while he returned to put the chain back on the bike. He then walked up and told this big shot that Jesus loved him. All five "tough guys" ran away.

Rick had poor teeth all his life. He saved money for several months to replace them. The old teeth were removed, and we all got to tease him about going toothless. Then, no Rick.

He dropped out of sight for nearly a month. A friend told me he was real sick from not eating because he didn't have any teeth. I knew he had the money for the new teeth and was long overdue for his appointment with the dentist.

It turned out that he gave away the money he had saved to a Christian woman who was hurting worse than he. She was about to lose her house so he gave her his denture funds. Talk about "find a need and fill it!" The church council quickly provided benevolence funds to pay for those teeth. We all felt it was one of the best investments we had ever made.

The Lord answered Rick's prayer about a godly wife, too. I'll never forget the night Tay Rainey stormed in. "Who is this Rick kid? He says he's going to marry my Nancy!" He no sooner calmed down then I had an upset Rick on my hands. I sent them to talk it out in the parking lot.

Half an hour later, Tay came back in grinning from ear to ear. "That young man submitted to me. He wants to marry Nancy, but only if I say so. He trusts God to speak through me."

When I asked what he told Rick, Tay got all weepy-eyed and whispered, "Of course it's all right if they marry."

The point is that God changed Rick drastically. He came to us, a very violent man. Then he became a tenderhearted Christian. Today he and Nancy have a stable marriage and lovely children; Rick has a great job; they own a home and twice have helped others plant new churches.

PASS ON THE GOOD NEWS!

Got time for one last "Rick story?" My friend Mike Faye was dating a girl named Cheryl Smalley. I hardly knew either of them at the time, but had prayed with Cheryl when she turned to the Lord. Mike wasn't yet a Christian, and he was a little skeptical of all that was going on. He was especially nervous when invited to an event called a "Hope Chapel Love Feast!" He barely got in the door when a certain biker wrapped him in an enormous bear hug. Rick informed this successful businessman and engineer that Jesus really loved him. Two days later, through tears, Mike asked the Lord into his heart. He said it was Rick's show of love that opened him up.

Jesus loved Will Heinle. Will passed it on to Rick, and Rick handed it off to Mike. That's evangelism in shoe leather.

Ralph and Ruby Moore shortly before their wedding. Automobile restoration would soon lead to restoration of souls.

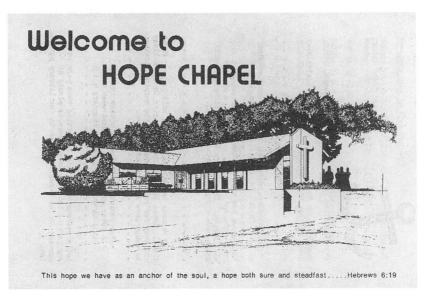

A bulletin cover picturing the original church building constructed to hold 60 people in the auditorium.

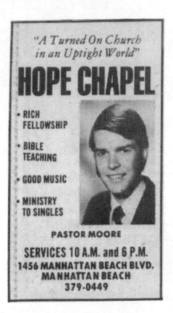

Original newspaper ad still shows Ralph in a suit. This ad appeared in the early weeks of Hope Chapel in Manhattan Beach.

In 1971 the original congregation of Hope Chapel Manhattan Beach could fit in a Volkswagen.

Mary Deriberprey was the only member remaining from the previous congregation which met in the building. She was a faithful member of Hope Chapel until her death in the late 1990s.

The Moore family, including Carl and Kelly, Christmas photo in 1975.

In 1974 this was a typical beach baptism. Will Heinle is at far right wearing a wet suit.

Bill Wilkinson, a member of Hope Chapel, opened a Christian bookstore.

A '70s style wedding at dawn on a Sunday morning.

Hope Chapel participants in Hawaii Summer Outreach. A street evangelism program sponsored by Kaimuki Christian Church and Pastor Harold Gallagher.

The original condition of the bowling alley. Immediately after the sale to Hope Chapel someone put up the sign announcing "God is Coming."

Craig Englert leading a home Bible study around the time we acquired the bowling alley. He later planted Hope Chapel Kihei, Maui.

Don and Pauline Stewart along with Richard and Ida Whittet. God sent these people to teach Ralph wisdom about management and leadership.

Staff Christmas photo in 1978, one year after the move to the new church building. Will Heinle would soon leave to pastor in Fallbrook, California.

Art and Carolyn Miller on a visit to Hawaii in 1998. They were the pastors in Granada Hills, California who sent us out to plant Hope Chapel in 1971.

In 1976, Bryon Koki, a young teen from Hawaii visited relatives in California. He accepted the Lord and we baptized him. He and his family were our first members in Hawaii and continue to play a vital role in the church.

6

LOVE AND UNITY

Any new church has several unique problems. One of which is a tendency for transplanted members to superimpose their previous church background and tradition on the rest of the congregation.

Most of our early members were "off-the-street" types, brand new to the church scene. But several people had a history in other churches. They brought their spiritual culture and tradition along with them. We were immediately left struggling with disunity in a very small church. Cliques and spiritual heritage groups quickly formed. Each had its own little set of "power plays" designed to corral me into someone else's ministry style.

They were all wonderful people. They operated with good intent. Most of these agenda-bearers had a solid background that they wanted to duplicate at Hope. However, they were wrong to force us into someone else's mold.

We had a group of people from Calvary Chapel. Another cluster came to us from The Church on the Way in Van Nuys. I was very open to the way their godly pastors, Chuck Smith and

Jack Hayford, did things. They were my mentors. But, I couldn't substitute either man for the Holy Spirit.

Another constituent group arrived from Melodyland Christian Center in Anaheim, California. The scene rounded out with a solid group of Christian bikers. They had grown up under the influence of a ministry called The Navigators. Finally, there were the other people, the ones who had only known me as their pastor. They had learned to trust the Lord and do as best they could without a lot of formal teaching, but they weren't incredibly solid.

I was pulled in four directions beside the one representing the style God was building into my own life.

LOVE MUST REIGN

The solution to our problem came from the pages of Paul's first letter to the Corinthian Christians. In Corinth, one group said, "We are of Paul." Another declared, "We are of Apollos." Still another claimed Cephas. The rest claimed they were of Jesus (1 Corinthians 1:10-29).

It is of utmost importance that the whole Church centers on Jesus rather than any man or ministry. The Christian church was not invented as a political platform. God works through individuals. He prefers the lowly to the high and mighty. His power displays itself best in our weakness. We would never solve our differences by argument of citing the plans of some favored leader. It was urgent that we stop struggling and seek direction from the Holy Spirit. Hope Chapel had a word from the Lord. He said he was planning a new work. We would never uncover his new idea in our state of disunity. If I gave in to any group and its identity, I would violate my mandate as pastor.

We studied Corinthians and understood the importance of unity. I realized that it was okay for each group to hold to the style that made them comfortable and to love their previous pastor. The important lesson was to accept each other. Rather than force any approach, we asked for the love of the brethren. They broke down and offered the love that marks true Christians.

Their love immediately freed me to recognize the various leaders of the existent groups. I could allow them to pastor the people already in their charge. Virgil Hemrick oversaw the biker types. Richard Agozino was definitely the leader of the Calvary folks, and so on. My role was defined as pastor to these pastors. I began to relate to leaders and did whatever I could to equip them. In one day I could easily telephone everybody in any leadership capacity, so communication was simple. We embraced our differences and celebrated the variety among ourselves. At the same time, we demanded love and respect for varying opinions.

I had to constantly remind myself that the Lord mattered, not Ralph Moore. I learned to trust God enough to trust the leaders he formed around me. The temptation was always to grab that ring of power, to want to control everything. Surrendering control of the church to the Lord of the church was key to our success. We could all work together because we were all willing to submit to the new direction God had for this church. We really were walking by faith.

Hope Chapel became an invading army. All platoons were united with a common purpose and identity, yet each was unique in approach. In a matter of weeks, though our Sunday attendance was much smaller, we were touching more than 200 people on a weekly average. Our Bible studies spread all over South Bay. We were in factories, hospitals, offices and schools. Some groups centered on prayer, others on didactic Bible study, while others majored in gifts of the Spirit. We all came together on Sunday to celebrate mutual victory. I taught eight studies each week. I led groups in homes and hospital cafeterias, as well as on the lawn at UCLA campus. Once, I was even attacked crossing a union picket line where I was to lead a Bible study at a missile factory. God thoroughly blessed these little bands of Christians at a time when most churches viewed off-campus Bible studies as "a tool of the devil." Our many Bible studies accomplished three things: (A) They caused spiritual growth in individuals. (B) They provided logistics to grow the number of people we could shepherd. (C) They gave the leaders a forum to develop pastoral abilities. Young leaders could test their skills and gifts without great risk. Several of those early leaders now pastor large churches. They learned the ministry by doing the ministry, much like the disciples of Jesus.

"THE" NEW THING

We never forgot those early prophecies the Lord sent to us. He had promised he was going to do something that we couldn't anticipate. We would sometimes question what in the world could the Lord do that we hadn't already seen. After all, Solomon said there is nothing new under the sun, everything has been done once. Solomon was right. God wasn't attempting anything new at all. His plan was simply so old that everyone had forgotten it.

God called our church to "mother" new churches. This was *the* new thing on our horizon. It had been a long time since anyone in our circles had sent pastors out to start new churches. It was even longer since they had worked with pastors trained in a local church through discipleship. The biblical pattern had been forsaken for at least two generations.

A Great Adventure

The New Testament is an adventure story: A great King was rejected and murdered by his people. Three days after the murder, he mysteriously appeared to his closest friends and colleagues. Forty days later, he sent them as emissaries to the whole world. They were to tell of his resurrection and accompanying message of eternal life. These men spread the news and planted cells of believers throughout the known world in one generation. Their accomplishment is one of the greatest success stories of all time.

Their strategy bears analysis. A dozen men with a world to conquer. All but one of them was executed for their effort. The lone exception was imprisoned for life; yet, they succeeded. So much so that an enemy once described them as those men who had turned the world upside down (Acts 17:6).

Trusting Naturally-Gifted Leaders

How did they achieve so much? The key was trust, both in God and men.

Wherever they went, they preached to whoever would listen. They had been instructed to brush off those who rejected their message (Matthew 10:12-14). Among those who believed, they quickly found *naturally gifted leaders,* appointing them to watch over the rest (Acts 14:23).

The apostles spent as little as three months in a single location. That meant men without formal education caught enough of Jesus to shepherd the flock in very little time. This seems a rash approach in a world filled with seminaries, libraries and denominational structures. But it worked! Today, churches possess multimillion dollar investments. Denominations control billions in real estate. The well-defined Christian establishment enjoys the best training tools and business strategy. However, we still long for the success of those early believers. It seems we've put too much trust in the institution and not enough in the Holy Spirit.

One Powerful Congregation

Actually, I grew up familiar with this very simple approach to evangelism. It lay at the center of my own denominational heritage. I grew up hearing the stories of the good old days in my larger church family. In the 1920s and '30s a church called Angelus Temple thrived in the Echo Park area of Los Angeles. This single congregation sent hundreds of men and women all over the world. Their task: Preach the gospel and plant new churches. Their in-house Bible institute offered only a three-month study program. Later it became a formal Bible college. But, even then, the school was heavy on ministry development with little academic emphasis. The result was churches sprouting around the world through these slimly-trained graduates.

As time progressed, institutionalism crept into the Foursquare movement along with the rest of the evangelical church. Everyone was in a holding pattern. The denomination expected to pioneer ministry through its headquarters. Meanwhile, the local church (which should have been raising and sending disciples) complained that not enough was happening.

They had lost the simple strategy of the Holy Spirit. Do you remember how he interrupted a local church prayer meeting to say, "Set apart for me Barnabas and Saul for the work to which I have called them?" (Acts 13:1-3). For, by the late 1940s, church- denominations, including mine, had usurped the Spirit's role as the calling agency. Their schools had co-opted the local church as a training vehicle. Church-planting ground to a halt. This is the world we faced when we planted our first *daughter church*.

We had discovered the Lord's "new (old) work" almost by accident.

He was right when he said, "Don't pray for it; you can't even anticipate it." Nothing in my background had ever challenged me to think of ordinary people in my congregation as the means to launching churches. We understood leadership development through discipleship but couldn't conceive of pastors trained in the local church. In fact, when we birthed the first daughter church, we got into trouble. Other pastors complained that we were somehow in rebellion to our denomination. They stirred up trouble even though we had the support of our national leaders.

BRANCH OF HOPE

Richard Agozino would change our understanding of New Testament strategies. Rich is one of the most courageous men I've ever known. As a young man he rode freight trains all over the United States. He worked for a while as a merchant seaman. He dabbled in drugs. Later, on a hot tip, he invested all his savings in gold stocks. That netted him enough money to buy a house.

He personified the term "radical" by living his convictions to their fullest. This young man attacked life with all he had. Then he met Jesus. He quickly went into high gear as a Christian. The guy advertised his faith with a huge sign covering the back window of his Volkswagen van. It read, "I'm a fool for Christ, whose fool are you?" Here was a person who had no problem with the biblical admonition to "love the Lord with all your heart, soul, mind and strength" (Mark 12:30). Rich was so turned on to the Lord that he was in church or teaching Bible studies nearly every night of the week. His family could hardly keep up with him.

Richard stormed into my life and into our congregation. His biggest Bible study group was looking for a home. They had outgrown several houses and moved into a nearby church. But because they spoke in tongues, the other church wasn't too interested in having them around. Some of his people scouted our church and felt that it would be a good place for the Bible study. They also liked us as a potential church home. Richard and I met one Wednesday afternoon so he could interview me. He put me on the hot seat with about a hundred questions about my past and what we believed. When I finally passed muster, he decided to lodge his group of followers in our congregation.

We soon became very close friends. Rich was preparing to go to New Zealand as a missionary. He was teaching Bible studies four nights a week, in addition to a full-time job as a finish carpenter, and his role as husband and parent. The straw that broke the carpenter's back was a fifth study group.

Meanwhile, several young families struggled to attend our Sunday evening service. It was difficult to get small children to bed after a long drive home from church. Our solution was to send church to them. Rich Agozino began leading Sunday evening services in a home in Torrance while the rest of us met in Manhattan Beach. The preparation and teaching load soon overwhelmed him. But, sometimes God has to put a person in a tight spot to get his attention.

Preparation for New Zealand was still underway when the two of us heard a man named Don MacGregor talk about church growth. Don was one of two American missionaries to the Philippines from our denomination. Under his leadership, a movement involving house churches and lay pastors spawned more than 55,000 converts a year. These people *lived* the Book of Acts.

Don spoke every night for a week, but it took only about 15 minutes for Agozino and I to decide his immediate future. New Zealand was out! South Torrance was in! Don spoke to our congregation in early October 1973. "Branch of Hope" (with Pastor Richard Agozino) held its first Sunday morning service the first week of December.

Twenty-five members of our 125-person church left to begin the new work. We learned something about letting go of the ring that day. We "let go" of 25 brothers and sisters. God sent 50 to replace them on the very day they left.

Rich quit his job and we helped the new church support him. He even supplemented his income with some of the equity from the sale of his house. The church met in a home for several months, then moved to a park. A few weeks under a picnic shelter brought considerable growth. Forced out of the park, they rented a defunct nightclub. When the City of Torrance put them out of the club, they returned to the park. This time, they won permission to use a recreation center.

Growth soon brought pressure for facilities. Rich used to take me on outings, looking for possible locations. We visited bank buildings, supermarkets, schools and whatever. They settled into a Seventh Day Adventist Church building for three years. Later they rented school buildings and were eventually able to lease a large church facility from another denomination.

That first daughter church grew more than 400 people. They also built and operated a boy's ranch and planted a couple of other congregations. God birthed his "new thing" through Richard Agozino. He taught us to plant churches and we've done it repeatedly ever since. Richard taught us to fulfill the prophecy by planting that first church. Richard went on to host *Crosstalk*, a Christian radio talk-show reaching audiences throughout Southern California.

7

FILLED AND OVERFLOWING

Branch of Hope wasn't the only church that had building problems. In 1971 Ruby and I planted the original Hope Chapel in a doll house. We had inherited a perfect miniature church building, almost a toy. It had classrooms designed for a teacher and two children. There were three classrooms plus an office and a nursery. Each of them had the same tiny, eight-foot by ten-foot, dimensions. Our auditorium maxed out at 72 people. Pink paint blanketed every wall with the exception of the lavender nursery. We still had no people, but knew the building just wasn't going to work.

We improvised. I taught the Bible in Sunday morning church. Everyone from junior high on up attended. Our Sunday school handled just the sixth graders and younger. We tore out walls, creating usable classroom space. Just by thinking differently, our tiny facility could accommodate a crowd three times larger than before. Because we had so few Sunday School classes, we freed ourselves from an oppressive teacher-recruitment problem. A shift in philosophy can very often save you money.

The building was quickly brimming with people. Since we couldn't stretch the building, we stretched our thinking. We packed 200 people into that little auditorium by knocking out the office and baptistery. Each week, we invited everyone in blue jeans to come sit on the rug surrounding me on the platform and on the floor all down the aisles. Special events demanded extra seating. Windows popped open to accommodate people sitting outside in the patio or on the lawn.

Parking was tougher. Our lot held just seven cars. We did everything that we could to maximize its use. Valet parking stretched it to cover 25 to 30 cars. We parked on the lawn behind the building. Eventually, we bussed people back and forth from a nearby parking lot.

Multiple services came next. Attendance doubled within weeks. The subsequent plan involved children's spaces. A nearby home purchase provided a downstairs garage for Sunday School and an upstairs apartment as a source of income. A very large lawn shed became an instant classroom for fourth graders.

Some generous people down the block rented us their nursery school for about two years. Their manager, though, resented the arrangement. She would call us every Monday morning to throw us out. She always claimed that we had left the place in a mess (we knew we hadn't). One of our men would go down the hill, calm her down and reinstate us. The owners were always on our side, the manager always against us. This went on for more than a year. Every week, we renegotiated ourselves back into that childcare center.

We did everything possible to exploit our small church building. Eventually, we topped out at 350 people on Sunday morning. Our facilities began to strangle vision and leadership.

Today, a church in the same position would simply rent a public school or community center and be done with their problems. In the early '70s, most communities and school districts were quite averse to renting to churches.

ROOM TO GROW

We struggled with local authorities. Over and over, we attempted to rent a community center two blocks from our church campus. The answer was repeatedly, "No." Meanwhile, another community center in the same town housed a thriving church. The city fathers didn't seem opposed to churches. This problem lay in the recreation department. Every time we talked to them, they would tell us that we couldn't use the center due to budgetary problems. We were told our money would go to the city treasury rather than the recreation department, but they would have to spend their own money to provide a custodian. Therefore, we couldn't use the building. Still, it didn't seem right that they rented to that other church.

This went on for more than four years. Eventually I ran into a former employee of the recreation department. She clearly stated that the budget story was merely a ruse to get us off their backs. Her suggestion: I should write the mayor asking if someone was taking money under the table from the church in the other community center. I did, with copies to the city manager and recreation director. Three days later, we had the lease agreement. The rec-center employees were cooperative and everything worked well from there on. We never really knew why we had been held off for so long. The recreation people seemed glad when we finally moved in.

We rented that building for about a year and a half, holding one service on Sunday morning and one on Sunday evening. An earlier service met up the hill in the little church building. The congregation grew to about 450 people. We filled all the chair space in the center and even had to seat people on tumbling mats stacked against the walls. Those mats provided real cushy "balcony" seating. Soon people were again outside looking through doors and windows. Frustration reigned eternal.

THE PROMISED LAND?

Five days after we moved to Manhattan Beach, I was startled by someone crawling through the church window. It turned out to be an old friend, Spencer Morris. Spencer and I were friends during our high school days in Portland. We dated the same girls, and had some great times together, though we were decidedly different.

Spencer was an independent thinker. He never graduated from high school because he skipped so many days of his senior year. He missed more than half a school year to do such exciting things as fishing. He was the first person who I ever rode with at more than a 100 miles an hour. Spencer always provided loads of excitement.

I moved away to college, and a year later he showed up. He passed the high school equivalency test. But he was the same old Spencer. He had fun while his school work suffered. He wasn't all that interested in what the teachers had to offer. However, he *was* interested in serving the Lord.

Well, I was cleaning the floor when Spencer came crawling through the window. I nearly suffered a stroke. He was in between jobs and looking for some excitement. He heard about our new church and decided to help. Actually, God sent him to show us the promised land.

Spencer moved into our house, and I hired him to clean the church, lead songs and preach whenever I was out of town. This was during the infancy of our church when the congregation numbered fewer than 20 persons. At that time, my wife and I could foresee a group numbering a couple of thousand people. Obviously, our building was too small to house the vision. Knowing this, Spencer found a place for us. He showed up one afternoon declaring, "I found the building, I know the place that God wants us to meet in for church."

He drove me up a hill to a huge and horribly vandalized piece of property. It had been built as a bowling alley in 1960 at a cost of $2 million. Eleven years later it lay waste. When the bowling business went bankrupt, the bank sold the pin setters and all other furnishings. It was just one large, empty room whose interior was one-third larger than a football field. Built on pillars, there was room for 120 cars beneath the structure.

We were certain we had found the "promised land." In fact, we were so certain that we publicly told people this was the place God provided for us. Our feelings were reinforced by three separate elderly people. Each had prayed when they noticed the structure going up a decade before. Their prayers were for God to turn it into a church. They had each felt that perhaps it was being built for a church. When they discovered it wasn't, they prayed that God would turn it into one.

SEEKING AN EYESORE

The vacant bowling alley had become a huge eyesore and a blight on the community. After researching the property for a year, we wrote the owners and invited them to donate it as a tax write-off. As you might guess . . . they didn't answer our letter.

As the months dragged on, the building became a sore spot for a couple of people in our church. They felt we should not grow, but remain small because churches belonged in homes or small, homey buildings. They couldn't relate to large, abandoned bowling alleys. The leadership, however, continued to feel that God had led us to this place.

We were constantly faced with the need for space and looked into a number of other properties also. We would get all excited, trusting the Lord for the bowling alley. We would pray for it, informing everyone in church that we were on our way to the promised land. When the owners would reject our offer, we'd grow depressed and look for other property. We repeated that cycle 19 times. Each time we returned to that defunct building as God's promise to us.

We angered four or five smaller churches when we asked if they would consider a swap. Industrial space and vacant super-markets were tempting, but out of reach. We once lost a race with the federal government for a huge warehouse. Both a high school and a junior high became our targets at separate times. You name it. We knew the size of the property and how much it cost. We knew everything about every chunk of land in the South Bay section of Los Angeles County. Finally, the search boiled down to either the bowling alley or Los Angeles Airport, nothing else worked. I guess you already know that no one was scrambling to sell us the airport.

I once got busted by the police while praying over that building. One night after a men's fellowship, Dick Whittet, Jim Suarez and I drove to the property to ask the Lord for it. There we were at 11:30 p.m. laying hands on this brick wall, praying that it would be ours. The police showed up. It seemed they frowned on that sort of activity. At least they were suspicious of such goings on after dark. With knees knocking and voices trembling, we explained what it was we were doing. They checked our ID and our story about Hope Chapel. Their response was, "Hope Chapel, huh. That's a good church. You get this building. We want you to have this building. We're tired of chasing kids through here in the middle of the night." Later, I read in a local newspaper that there had been a couple of rapes in the building, and that a policeman had been murdered in what is now called the Ocean View Room.

BOWLING ALLEY AND A COCONUT TREE

I remember attending a pastors' conference in Colorado, praying my heart out that God would give us the building. There were 1,100 people in this auditorium when the speaker asked us to turn to somebody we knew and pray with them. As I turned around, Jack Hayford grabbed both my wife and me. He then spoke a word of prophesy to us. I don't remember his exact words. But let me paraphrase, "The Lord has established you as a tall coconut tree, standing on a hill overlooking the ocean. Don't think it strange that the Lord has compared you to a coconut tree. It's a very natural thing for a coconut tree to give off coconuts which grow into daughter trees, and the Lord will establish your comings and your goings." The significance of that prophecy was yet to be understood, but it now seems the Lord was talking to us about establishing churches in the illustration of the coconut. The emphasis was on reproduction, but I missed it.

I believed that Jack had spoken a word from the Lord to us. But, I could only focus on the part about this coconut tree planted on a *hill* by the ocean. That bowling alley was on a hill overlooking the Pacific Ocean in Hermosa Beach.

A DISMAL AUCTION

Upon returning from the convention, I sat down and read the *Los Angeles Times*. In fact, I read through the previous 13 copies of the *Los Angeles Times* that had piled up while we were gone. Since I'd paid for them, I was going to read them. Meanwhile, Ruby browsed the ads, clipping coupons. She came upon an advertisement describing several buildings at auction. Among them was our favorite bowling alley!

You have to understand how we felt. Just two days earlier Pastor Hayford had prophesied about us being planted on a hill overlooking the ocean. Then my wife suddenly discovered the building was up for auction. We were absolutely certain that God would give us the building at auction. The timing of the prophecy and of the newspaper discovery was no coincidence. The building was ours.

That Sunday I preached on Israel entering the promised land. The church held a special prayer meeting. We felt that the days of wandering around in the wilderness were coming to an end. The doors were finally opening, and we were moving to *our* promised land.

At that time, we were introduced to a man named Norman Hahn who had excellent credentials in real estate. He received an award from Governor Reagan in 1973. That year he sold more real estate than any other person in California. His resume reflected the sale of an entire town, including an airport. He was also a wonderful Christian. Our leadership team was very young. We barely understood business, but felt we could safely trust this man. He was worthy of our trust. He gave us good advice and spent hours on our project as a ministry to us. There were 400 of us in church on Sundays. But we had no money in the bank. Every dime in the offerings was either spent on ministry or given to someone in need. We were giving away 30 percent of our income. Lack of reserves birthed panic. We feared committing ourselves to the building with resources so tight. Our denominational supervisor, Paul Jones, and Mr. Hahn helped us rearrange our priorities around the needs of Hope Chapel. We had been too bent on giving money away. We had failed to ensure the future of the congregation. Those men informed us that if we couldn't house the church, there would be no funds to give to the needy.

We calculated some cutbacks and projected the ability to make payments. The building had cost nearly $2 million to build years earlier. It had been for sale for more than $400,000. However, Norm felt that we could buy it for a quarter of a million at the auction. We had no way to touch that kind of money by ourselves. The Foursquare people came to our rescue. Dipping into their home missions fund, they gave us a certified check for 15 percent of the $250,000 which was $37,500. This would tie up the property while they arranged a loan for us for the balance. Looking back, this all seems like pennies, but it was serious cash in 1975.

Despair loomed tall and ugly at the auction. Excitement and panic tangled like two TV wrestlers as the auctioneer set up his little table in front of the building. The parking lot billowed with bidders, onlookers, and about a hundred Hope Chapel folks on a prayer mission. At exactly ten o'clock the auctioneer brought down his gavel and opened the bidding.

The first and last bid was for $275,000. Twenty-five thousand more than our prearranged limit. A local entrepreneur and land developer planned to build racquetball courts in place of bowling lanes.

We were losers, locked out of our promised land. I cried in the alley behind the supermarket. I can remember exactly where I sat on the steps of the Lucky Market loading dock. With swollen eyes, I watched a tall man in a blue suit walk beyond the cyclone fence. In slow motion, he pushed back broken glass doors, and hiked up the steps to survey his purchase.

FEELING THE FOOL

I was a fool. I would go back to the congregation and explain that I had led them down a primrose path to nowhere. I was a prophet who didn't know what he was talking about. We'd wound up with nothing but empty words.

I was so devastated that I avoided that building every time I could help myself. I didn't even want to look at it. My wife and I would go far out of our way to keep from driving past the intersection. Sometimes I found myself an unwilling passenger in the neighborhood. I would turn my head. Crippling feelings of emptiness and self-doubt held the day. My kids loved McDonald's, about a block away. I'd sit with my back to the structure—the roof was visible from McDonald's.

Feeling the fool, I dove into the Scriptures. I related to David running from Saul. First, David had believed God was going to make him king in Jerusalem. King Saul tried to murder him and David ran for his life. He then saw himself as a hunted flea certain of his own impending destruction (1 Samuel 26:20). I could identify with David.

I need to confess that during those dark days I was simply feeling sorry for myself. I wanted control of my life and circumstances. I felt that God had trusted me with a message and that I had faithfully passed it on to others. Now I was left holding the empty bag. I raged against the possibility that I could be wrong. God had taken control of circumstance away from me and it was painful, nearly disastrous. I felt like quitting the pastorate. I wished I could die. All this pouting merely pointed out what a good grasp I had on that *ring* we've discussed throughout this book. The Bible record is very consistent. God forces everyone he blesses to relinquish the ring of power before he does his part. We cannot be gods unto ourselves and expect him to work in our situation.

My real problem was personal selfishness. Our people needed that bowling alley for a house of worship. My position was a little different. I lusted for it to validate my perspectives. I wanted to say, "I told you so. I was right all along." I don't think God was too thrilled by my attitude.

PRAY "UNTIL"

As I look back, the strangest part of the whole experience is that the building kept crowding into my thoughts. I managed to find that old bowling alley everywhere in Scripture. I knew all those Bible heroes suffered loss of face before inheriting God's success. God first made promises to Abraham when he was 75-years-old. He waited nearly a quarter of a century to receive a promised son. At 98 he laughed in God's face and tried to teach him the genetic facts of life. He knew the impossibility and tried to prove it. Joseph not only waited for God's promise, he spent the time in jail as an accused rapist. Jeremiah's peers saw him as a traitor and false prophet. I guess I didn't have things so bad. But, the stories of these men and others like them were hard to handle. They continually prompted me to believe when I wanted to give up. The entire experience was negative and I wanted it behind me. However, those Old Testament patriarchs and prophets wouldn't give up. They seemed to scream out, "Trust him just a little longer!"

We weren't able to give up praying for this building! My friend Roy Hicks once taught that we should learn to pray "until." In other words, we should pray until God comes through. We should never give up on him. "Until" can feel like a very long time.

During the months after the auction I felt painfully *called* to trust God for the building. I was exhausted and fought the call. At least the future would be predictable if we gave up hope. Yet, the Holy Spirit prevailed and many of us continued to ask for that building. We eventually found peace with the God whom we could not control.

BREAKTHROUGH

Santa Barbara is wonderful in the fall. The summer haze past, the whole town shimmers in the cool, autumn sun. We went there to pray for direction. Each fall the pivotal leaders in our church would take time for a prayer retreat and return with plans for the future. Someone spoiled the meeting when they spoke the obscene words *bowling alley*.

A month earlier, we'd laughed over the news that the city wouldn't allow the racquetball courts due to a structural problem. We rejoiced that day, but the tears flowed when we tried to buy it from the new owner. He wouldn't work with us. The grapevine informed us that he was going to leave the building alone and untouched. It would remain a vandalized monument to the bureaucracy that overturned his sports complex. Whatever his reasons, he wouldn't deal with us. Norm Hahn would show up with an offer. The owner would promise to consider it and respond in a couple of days. His response was to raise the price or not call back at all.

When someone in our prayer meeting said "bowling alley," the rest looked like they were ready to pack up, head for Los Angeles and forget the retreat. It didn't turn out that way.

We talked awhile and prayed intensely one afternoon. That evening we worshiped him in song. God gave us the plan we sought that night. God says that in all our ways we are to acknowledge him and he will direct our paths (Proverbs 3:5-6). As we did that through song and praise, he came roaring through on our behalf.

God spoke to my heart, suggesting that we enter into a different style of negotiation. We were to approach the owner and ask him if he would sell us the property, but allow him to name the final sales price. The deal would stand or fall on his words.

Let me tell you how it worked. I visited my parents on vacation that summer. While I was there, my dad bought a set of snow tires for his pickup truck. He found them advertised in the newspaper, and went out to visit the man who owned them. He looked over the tires and found that they were in very good condition, almost new. He asked the man, "What's the lowest price you're willing to take? You name the price, and I'll go ahead and pay you that for the tires." The whole deal depended upon a trust that my father had built in this man in just a few moments time. Dad felt he could believe in him so he said, "I'll pay your price," even before he knew what it was. The man sold him the tires at a very favorable price. I must point out that the guy really had my father over the barrel. If he had been unscrupulous, we would have been in an embarrassing situation.

God told us to approach our "promised land" bowling alley in exactly the same manner as my father had bought the tires.

Our church council wrote a letter to that effect and I signed it. The letter began: "Dear Sir: This is the most unusual letter you'll ever read. . . ." We went ahead to promise this man that we would buy his property at whatever price he named. He would name the price and then say these words, "This is the lowest amount I'm willing to take for the property." Because our denomination covered us with veto power, we couldn't get into too much trouble with the offer. There was no way we could be held to a contract with a really ridiculous price. However, if the price was in the ballpark, we were committed to the project.

We were so intent on vulnerability and trust that we sent along financial statements covering our entire history. We wanted this man to know exactly where we stood.

A NEW FRIEND

A couple of weeks later, I got a telephone call. The owner misread our motives. He thought that we were up to some trick and were trying to cheat him out of the building. When we began to understand each other, he got excited and decided to try and find a way to glean a tax advantage by donating it to our church.

In two days, he came back with an opportunity for us to buy the property at only $175,000, if we could move within 30 days. He would take a great tax loss on the property and it would benefit us.

We didn't have the ability to move that fast. So, he conjured up a better plan. This one would fly. Things had so turned around since that prayer meeting that the formerly reluctant owner now became a good friend.

He worked out a lease with an option to purchase. This came at a time when real estate prices were moving like a rocket. It was a sellers' market and lease options were simply not available. He could have simply held the property and made money any time he decided to sell.

He generously allowed us to lease for up to two years, with an option to purchase for only $350,000. He had lowered his most recent asking price by $150,000. The payments were easy for us to work with. Within months of that prayer meeting we began to remodel our new home.

The remodeling was done by faith. We signed the lease with only $4,000 in the bank and cash flow barely adequate to make the lease. In our naivete, we estimated that it would cost $30,000 to remodel the building. It wound up costing 10 times that much.

The Lord worked gracious wonders. The least of which was to supply the necessary money. Also, the crew were miracle workers. We hired five church members as full-time remodelers. If volunteers came, one or two of them would break off to supervise. This plan allowed very intelligent use of untrained volunteer labor. As a result, our labor costs came in at 20 percent of the undertaking. They're usually above 50 percent on any similar project.

Every week we took in huge offerings, but they never contained huge checks. It was just that a lot of people gave more than they ever had before. Our offerings contained surplus funds right up to the day we moved in. We canceled the lease, and bought the property six months after driving the first nail.

A LITTLE TOO COCKY

Our first Sunday at the new location attracted lots of attention. Our story made the *South Bay Daily Breeze*. The *Los Angeles Times* did a full-page story, and NBC television covered "The Church in a Bowling Alley" with a three-and-one-half minute nationwide feature. Friends and family phoned and wrote from all over the country. They had seen us on TV and we soon felt more important than we were.

We got cocky, but the Lord was prepared for us. The huge offerings dropped right back to normal. This was bad news. For, although we had a "Certificate of Occupancy," we hadn't yet completed the construction.

There was another complication. We had set out to buy carpet from a legitimate carpet company. We would enjoy a discount since the owner was a friend of one of our members. A little later, we came across a "better deal" at a little hole-in-the-wall carpet shop in nearby Venice. The man asked for the entire payment in advance. However, when the carpet arrived from the mill it was marked "Collect on Delivery."

We weren't confused for very long. We soon discovered that the carpet dealer had stolen our money. He gave us a sob story about how his morals were corrupted because he'd been detained by Nazis during the Holocaust in World War II. He used the money to pay some other expense. We actually fell for his story. He seemed helpless. We even got him to pray for forgiveness and to accept the Lord. Then our attorney discovered that he had transferred his business and home into his son's name so we couldn't touch them. Someone from another church had told him to pray with us. They promised him that we wouldn't sue him if he became a Christian. Wrong! We did win a judgment against him. But there was no way to touch his assets. He just took us to the cleaners.

There was one upside to all our financial woes. God used them to humble us. For weeks we held church in very depressing circumstances. There was no carpet on the floor, no paint on the walls and no money to buy either. It was worse than you might imagine. Lack of carpet produced a horrible slapping echo. Worship and teaching suffered badly. The problems, however, erased the pride induced by our three-and-a-half minutes of fame. We got off our high horse, learning to trust and pray again. Of course, the Lord supplied our need.

8

MINICHURCH

"They entered the promised land and lived happily ever after." That statement wasn't true in ancient Israel, and it surely didn't describe us. We really thrashed around after the move into the new facility. First, we had the financial crisis and found ourselves up to our Bibles in red ink. Second, we lost our focus. We were driven off our mission by new people attracted to what had become a very beautiful location. In each case, the Lord sent a solution that gave us more strength than we had before we encountered the problem.

A FINANCIAL MESS

Both problems came from inexperience. The financial mess was born of a leadership team long on faith and love, but weak in resource management. We hadn't tracked our spending and now we were in trouble. Big trouble! When we discovered the problem, we needed an amount equal to the price of a small house just to pay local hardware and building suppliers. Salaries weren't even up for consideration.

The Lord came through from three directions: (A) A young captain of a merchant ship gave us an ocean-view lot he had purchased for his dream home. The equity met half our need. (B) The Foursquare denomination gave us a cash gift and a loan, completing the bailout. (C) The third blessing was a man named Don Stewart. Don spent his early life in aerospace engineering and management. He helped us as a board member but soon resigned from secular work to join our pastoral team. He soon ironed out our financial woes, then taught us to manage both people and money. He grew to function as our anchor of stability. God used Don to ensure the success of many grand schemes that might have failed without his godly insights and wise restraint.

RESPECTERS OF PERSONS

Financial needs are one thing, pride problems are quite another. In our early days people scoffed at "that bunch of hippies" and wouldn't associate with us. Now we were in the limelight and socially acceptable. They joined and our attitudes deteriorated. One day I noticed several Mercedes and Cadillacs where the crusty Volkswagens had previously parked. Someone was even driving a Rolls-Royce to our church. We had simply grown to a stage where we could minister to a broader range of people. They liked us the way we were, but we didn't get it. We thought we had to change to appeal to people of means. I remember discussing image and impression with one of our staff guys. We decided to take a little more "uptown" approach to ministry. We needed class.

Remember Jesus? He said that he would build his church and that pastors should feed the sheep. Well, I took over his role and schemed to build the church. Before that day, image and appearance meant very little to any of us in leadership. It all too quickly became very important.

We had exploded with growth for a few weeks after the move. Then I took over, and we started losing. I usurped the Lord's place, grabbed onto that "ring of control" and wouldn't let go. We then "grew" from 800 people to 600 and holding.

No one even stopped to consider that all the new people had come because the Lord sent them. We never considered that they wanted what we had to offer by just being ourselves. They would have kept coming if we held steadfastly to our ministry pattern. Instead, we generated elaborate, new programs to hold people and bind them in.

The Kentucky Fried Chicken people proudly declare, "We do chicken right." They imply that they are the best at chicken because they don't dilute their efforts with every other fast food. We used to "do equipping right," but we abandoned that role for everything we could conceive that would cause growth. When we lost our focus, we did nothing right.

There is a clear pattern in the New Testament for church growth. The elders reinforce themselves by "devoting themselves to prayer and the Word (Acts 6:4)." Then those leaders become a gift to the church to "equip God's people to do his work" (Ephesians 4:11-13). This equipping goes on as the church meets regularly for teaching, fellowship, breaking of bread (communion) and prayer. Strengthened in the Spirit, the individual Christians penetrate, flavor, preserve, and influence their culture. As the Christians live an overcoming life among their friends, the Lord adds new people to the congregation on a daily basis (Acts 2:47). We ignored that plan for several years.

Sure, we could describe it in glowing terms, but we didn't practice what we preached.

Because of our history, people were researching our "rapid growth" for doctoral dissertations. I regularly spoke at church growth institutes and seminars. The problem? Our story was only fading history. We weren't growing in numbers. I believe it's only hypocritical to say we grew spiritually during that time. Healthy sheep breed more sheep. Had we been healthy, our numbers would have increased. We got our eyes off of people and onto facilities, then onto a program.

After languishing for two years, we finally got back on track. The solution to this problem also strengthened us, immeasurably.

ON THE REBOUND

I gave up trying to pastor a "big church" and went back to being myself. I prayed for direction, and the Lord told me to tend his flock. Problem was, I didn't even know the flock. People could attend for many months only to be recognized as newcomers. There was no network of personal relationships. It wasn't so bad if I didn't recognize people. But it was just awful that no one did. We began to understand that we needed a small-church mentality. We would have to subdivide the congregation to get it.

1) Big Church—Small Church

The goal was to start a network of house meetings to reflect on the teaching from the previous weekend services. This would make us a more faithful representation of the apostle's model, involving meetings in the temple and from house to house (Acts 2:46). We could be a big church that offered the support and intimacy enjoyed by small congregations. We had enjoyed such a model in our early years in Manhattan Beach. Weekend church was followed by all those Bible studies. Over the years we gravitated into a large model with me doing most of the teaching. We saw the need and the pattern. But how would we make the switch? Three past attempts to revive small groups were proven failures.

One day, Craig Englert, one of our pastors, came in all excited about something going on in a little church we helped start in Honolulu. The three pastors had divided the congregation into three groups, and on Sunday night they met in separate homes for Bible studies. They had replaced a *regularly scheduled church service* with small groups. It worked well. As people got to know each other, they ministered to each other almost spontaneously. They learned to serve each other in a relaxed atmosphere of love and acceptance. The Honolulu church leaders felt their success lay in the schedule they chose. They used a time slot already well accepted by their congregation as a time for church. This was at a time when most churches still held Sunday evening worship services. Their folks simply switched venues on a night they were used to coming to church.

2) Unity of Purpose

We gathered the leaders of our congregation for a church growth conference at one of our daughter churches. John Amstutz, on staff at LIFE Bible College and Fuller Theological Seminary, helped us assess the strengths and weaknesses of our church. After individually grading Hope Chapel in seven categories of church health, we gathered to discuss our ratings. It was nearly unanimous that we needed a small group encounter in the middle of the week. Our people needed an opportunity to share their problems and victories. They needed to get to know one another. The small groups should replace a regular service like they had done in Hawaii. The schedule would work for more than reasons of convenience. It would also signal our seriousness about the venture.

We prayed for a week, then had a meeting of what I called the "undershepherds." This included everybody I could identify as any kind of leader in our church. We involved 150 of our 600 people. The only criterion for leadership was that a person had a follower. Even the church rebels received an invitation. If a person could influence another, we assumed that they were using (or abusing) a God-given ability. This forced us to recognize spiritual gifts whether they were used in a godly fashion or not. These people were, in fact, shepherding the flock alongside of me. Talk about surrender; I had to admit I wasn't the whole show.

At the meeting we presented a proposed solution to our problem. Our church staff and two other men would lead the initial groups. The groups would be called *MiniChurches,* or miniature churches. They would function along the lines of Paul's admonition to the Corinthians. Everyone was expected to participate actively in each meeting (1 Corinthians 14:26). They would be miniature churches, focused on each person's needs and potential. The pastor would be the coach, the people would move out of the stands and onto the field. They would function as players, ministering to one another (Romans 15:14). Worst case: Someone would know your name if you came to our church and joined a MiniChurch.

3) MiniChurch Rocks!

We were back where we started. I pastored pastors and recognized that they pastored the church. It worked before, and it worked even better when we revived it. Our attendance jumped from 85 to 365 in one week. We moved from one teacher in a single midweek meeting to seven leaders in seven separate home groups. Better yet, each MiniChurch "shepherd" was instructed to raise up a couple of apprentices. We were on the road to multiplication of leadership. The MiniChurch became an on-the-job training center for a new generation of pastoral leadership.

4) Needs and Hunger

The advent of MiniChurch spotlighted needs and hungers we didn't realize existed within our congregation. Our people craved community. MiniChurch provides it. Today between 50 and 60 percent of a Hope Chapel congregation attend Mini-Church. We still think of them as a midweek phenomenon. In reality, the groups meet at all hours and on every day of the week. I even know of a MiniChurch that gathers from 10 p.m. to midnight on Fridays.

EARLY CHURCH "ARCHITECTURE"

Form and function are always intertwined. The ideal is for form to follow function. In other words, how we do things is always driven by purpose. I believe this was as true for the earliest Christians as it is for us in the third millennium. They met and worshiped in borrowed facilities. But if they chose the facilities, they selected them to fit the purpose behind their meetings. On the day of Pentecost, the church began with 120 members. By the end of the day, there were 3,000 additional converts. The crowd now numbered at least 3,120 people. They met in Solomon's Porch in the Jewish Temple in Jerusalem (Acts 5:12), and in the homes of their members. Archaeology reveals that the temple area would have housed roughly 400 persons. The houses would max out at less than a dozen. The sizes of the meeting spaces differed in a way that would affect the type of activity held in each. Big spaces work best for large crowds with a single focus. In large groups most people remain spectators. Small rooms accommodate a family atmosphere with lots of interchange and participation. I believe those early Christians heartily embraced both settings *because* each offered its own possibilities. The second chapter of Acts outlines the basic activities of the early church. They were teaching, fellowship, breaking bread (shared meals and holy communion), prayer, praise, sharing of material goods, and evangelism. The first six of these took place inside the church. The seventh, evangelism, occurred among the neighbors in the outside community. Let's take a look at how each of these activities work best in either the large (temple) or the small (homes) setting.

Architecture of the
New Testament Church

"Solomon's Portico"
(Large weekend meetings)

"House meetings"
(Mid-week meetings)

✓	Teaching	✓
	Fellowship	✓
	Breaking Bread	✓
	Prayer	✓
✓	Praise	
	Sharing/Giving	✓
	Evangelism	

The second chapter of Acts outlines the basic activities of the early church. They were teaching, fellowship, breaking bread (shared meals and holy communion), prayer, praise, sharing of material goods, and evangelism. The first six of these took place inside the church. The seventh — evangelism — occured among the neighbors in the outside community.

1) Teaching

We would agree that professional teaching works best in the temple or large-group setting. One person invests heavily in message preparation. They then skillfully present their material to a large-group of people massed in rows of chairs or pews.

The arrangement is *efficient* because it accommodates so many people for an enlightened presentation. However, the same teaching grows more *effective* if it includes an interactive element. This is where the small group comes in. When people interact with a lesson, they tend to absorb it. Our MiniChurches provide an "application laboratory" for dissecting and living the truth taught in the pastor's weekend message.

This type of Bible study allows for questions to connect with answers. People can express opinions and challenge each other's thinking. There is time to search through the side roads and back alleys of the Bible for deeper understanding. Each size provides its own unique benefit.

2) Fellowship

This one is a hands down winner in a MiniChurch. Most large-group experiences allow for little more than a quick hello and a handshake. The small group often includes tears, and follow-up telephone calls. There is adequate time to fully know others and become known by them. The Greek New Testament references fellowship with the term *koinonia*. It more literally translates, "partnership." With families crumbling, the MiniChurch sustains people with partnering friendships that sustain them through life's storms. The bonds of those friendships grow by spending lots of time together in a warm and relaxed setting.

3) Breaking Bread

Some would see these words pertaining to holy communion and nothing else. Others would restrict communion to the large setting under the leadership of an ordained member of the clergy. For them, breaking bread simply takes the form of potluck suppers. I believe both holy communion and shared meals were covered by the term "breaking bread." Both function well in either the large or small group. But for my purposes holy communion works best in the large group. There it usually entails sober reminders of the great lengths of God's love and forgiveness. Just eating together is a small group function. A potluck builds family feelings into a group of relative strangers. We get into the food pretty well. We actually *begin* our MiniChurch meetings with food. Eating together forces us to take time for fellowship. Sharing food opens people to one another. The time spent eating together gives opportunity to catch up on each others lives since the last time we met. It also provides a buffer for people who show up a few minutes after we start. Late arrivals can slip in without disrupting the Bible study. Finally, it provides an appetite suppressor for the person coming directly from the workplace.

4) Prayer

Sorry, but large group prayer experiences leave me cold. Large prayer settings become spectator sports. One performs. The others simply listen. I much prefer to pray with a few intimate friends. In the smaller setting, we have a better shot at "agreeing" in prayer (Matthew 18:19-20).

The prayer results in our MiniChurches are quite amazing. We think it is for three reasons: (A) We pray over *felt* needs, not "prayer requests." If a problem is really important, it will spill out during the fellowship, Bible study and discussion. Praying this way tends to keep us focused on the immediate lives of our members, not their workmates, cousins or Aunt Jenny's cat. (B) We take time to pray. The last part (20 minutes to half hour) of the meeting is devoted to prayer. By praying for someone during that time, our members are also implying a promise to pray for them until our next meeting. (C) We follow up with praise reports. Our food and fellowship sessions at the beginning of each meeting usually center on the previous week's prayer requests. Positive results build greater faith.

5) Praise and Worship

It may surprise you, but I favor leaving praise and worship out of the small group. For one thing, we sing praises much better in a crowd. Auditoriums filled with people generate enthusiasm and excitement. Skilled worship teams *teach* worship and *lead* us into meaningful time with God. I love to sing God's praises with the whole congregation in attendance.

The informality of the small group works against this kind of praise-giving. People often request favorite songs which can lead to an unfocused experience. Neighbors complain when the singing gets louder. Worship can take over the schedule and other important business gets left unfinished. I've been in Bible study groups that never studied the Bible, because they got caught up in worship. That is not a bad thing as long as it remains the exception rather than the rule.

Short schedules and important priorities cause our MiniChurches to focus on the Scriptures and prayer. Praise finds expression in testimonies of God's life-changing power through both.

6) Giving and Sharing Resources

Weekend worship celebrations provide the best setting for financial offerings to the church. They offer security and well-thought usage of the collected monies. Small groups can, however, sometimes direct resources toward an individual member in ways the larger organization could not. In our churches, benevolence giving is tied to the recommendation of the MiniChurch leader. The monies come from the church treasury, but only after referral from the small group.

MiniChurches have other resources to offer. Household items and used cars often change hands as gifts within a fellowship group. We sometimes discover people giving significant sums of money to a friend in need. The need became known through MiniChurch. Several widows have had their homes renovated as a project of their small group. These acts of generosity tie people together. They also impress nonChristian onlookers.

7) Evangelism

The earliest Christians lived dangerous lives. Officially outlawed, they were persecuted and even killed for their faith. Shortly they began meeting in secret. Secrecy didn't do much for public advertising or great public events designed to bring people to Jesus. For these reasons, most people came to Christ through the testimony of a friend. Acts chapter two says these Christians enjoyed favor with their number. As a result, God added to their number daily. Changed lives impress even the greatest religious skeptics.

The Holy Spirit authors the changes. His tools are the lives of people equipped and strengthened through a healthy church experience. He uses all of the above elements. Having both large *and* small group tools makes his job somewhat easier.

9

VISION

Hope Chapel Hermosa Beach really got moving after the introduction of MiniChurch. Watching its rising momentum was a bittersweet experience for me. While I enjoyed God's blessing on the church, a new awareness of mission came crawling into my heart. Orders arrived dictating service in a new location.

Dick Whittet, one of our pastors, and I were walking near the beach in May 1978. He told me the Lord had asked him to pray for me every day. Dick and his family were preparing to plant a Hope Chapel in Bozeman, Montana, at the time. He told the Lord, "Ralph should be praying for me, instead." The Lord assured him I needed the prayer support. Dick just wanted me to know he was praying.

Six weeks later I took my family on vacation to Hawaii. As I walked up the aisle of the airplane (if you must know, I was headed for the restroom), I saw a vision. Now, I'm not a person given to visions. I don't seek these experiences as I believe God usually communicates through the inner voice of the Holy Spirit. And, being somewhat skeptical, I'd probably doubt you if you said you'd seen one. Nevertheless, I saw a vision.

During the brief experience, it was as though I was in three places at once. I was alert to my position in the plane. But, I could also envision *myself* in the clouds looking down upon *myself* standing among a number of mostly black-haired people. We were standing on the mountainside above Kaneohe, Oahu. Strangely, I seemed to be in all three places at once.

Also, sizes seemed out of proportion. The people, myself included, were of normal size. The town and the beautiful bay seemed shrunken to about one-third the size of a football field.

Two terms came to mind: *dominant* and *five years*. I questioned the word "dominant" as descriptive of any ministry. We are supposed to be servants. The "five years," though, seemed an indication that I was to live out the picture five years later.

The entire vision could not have taken more than three seconds. I immediately dismissed it as momentary hysteria.

I felt God had called me to spend my whole life with a group of people in California identified as Hope Chapel Hermosa Beach. Furthermore, visions can be misleading—especially to a person that loves Windward Oahu for its wet, green beauty. Another confusing element was the fact that I had spent the previous week with 1,200 Japanese-American Christians. A group called JEMS (Japanese Evangelical Missionary Society) had invited me to teach at their annual summer camp. I feared that their love and kindness might be causing this unusual spiritual experience.

I knew the so-called vision had to be a trick of my psyche or worse. Maybe the devil was trying to distract me from the work the Spirit was doing in Hermosa. I forgot the whole thing. I forgot it so well that I hardly remembered it when Dick Whittet brought it up at the end of my vacation.

REFRESHING A MEMORY

We were gone for three weeks, and flew the *red eye* home so we could squeeze in an extra five hours at the beach. The plane landed at six a.m. Friday. Fourteen hours later, I would be in the pulpit. Unable to sleep, I went to the church around noon to open my mail. Tired and grumpy, I encountered Dick as I was leaving for dinner. He asked, "Did anything unusual happen on your trip? Remember, I've been praying for you. The Lord told me that on your vacation you would be lifted up in the air and given a vision of your future."

I laughed him off. I looked at my watch and said, "It's four o'clock. My vacation is officially over at seven, so if God has any visions for me, he'd better hurry!"

At about 6:10 p.m. it all came back. Badly shaken, I dropped the peas off my fork. Dick had just described the vision I had seen three weeks earlier. I had been *lifted up,* both literally and figuratively. Flying at 25,000 feet, I had felt myself hovering in the clouds over Kaneohe Bay. On the mountainside below, God painted a picture of my future. I found Dick and apologized for my smart attitude. I also swore him to secrecy.

My master's program at California Graduate School of Theology required a thesis. It provided opportunity to research the spiritual situation in Hawaii. Unable to cover the entire population, I wrote nearly 200 pages called "A History of Christianity Among Japanese-Americans in Hawaii." This process gave me wonderful background on the new challenge.

I still told no one about the vision except Ruby and my friend, Aaron Suzuki. Aaron was raised both in Hawaii and on the mainland. Before coming to the Lord, he spent nights and weekends experimenting with drugs and a pretty fast lifestyle. By day, he excelled as an engineer at American Honda. Having found emptiness in life's pleasures, Aaron was also planning suicide. The afternoon of the "big day," he asked Jim Doehla, a charismatic Lutheran and co-worker, why he was so happy. Jim told him about God's love offered through Jesus Christ. He also gave him a pocket-sized copy of the Book of Romans from the New Testament. Aaron hid in a lavatory stall at Honda and read through the entire thing. Though he understood little of the message, he sensed God's love. Today he laughingly describes his mixture of tears and hope as he read words he barely under- stood. Later that evening, Aaron found new life. Jim led him in a prayer to invite the Lord into his life. Instead of committing suicide, Aaron was born again that night.

Jim thought Aaron too "hip" to fit into his own traditional Lutheran church. Instead, he brought him to a Hope Chapel baptism on New Year's Eve, 1973. They *both* immersed them- selves in our church. These two very different individuals, like unmatched bookends, became great support for many people.

By 1978 Aaron felt God might be calling him to pastor, particularly among Japanese-Americans. Maybe in Hawaii. When I shared the vision, he *didn't* think I was crazy. He even read through my very long master's thesis. Along with our wives, we invested much prayer into the possibility of moving. Soon we were assured that God was calling us to Hawaii to plant churches.

BITTERSWEET ADVENTURE

New challenges are always exciting, and I thrive on adventure, but this endeavor involved the pain of leaving dear friends and familiar circumstances. Bittersweet indeed.

Ken Hiroshige hit me with his wisecrack about letting go of the ring a little prematurely. Since he didn't attend our church, I told him about the move fairly early—long before I announced it in church. It was also long before I could feel the pain, so his comment seemed unreal. It actually signaled a great struggle. The church grew 250 percent in the years immediately following the establishment of MiniChurch. The growth made leaving harder on both the heart and ego.

We planted churches from Hawaii to Montana to Texas during those few years. Several of them started churches in their neighboring localities. I said goodbye to many friends. Dave Benefiel went to Moorpark, California. Dick Whittet to Montana. We lost Will Heinle to Fallbrook, California; Barry Felis went to Huntington Beach; Dan Boyd planted Hope Chapel Del Rey in Westchester, California.

A couple of years before we moved to Hawaii, Craig Englert started Hope Chapel Kihei, Maui. Meanwhile one of his disciples, Gregory Koukl, began a radio broadcast that now airs from coast to coast. From Kihei, Englert and company planted three daughter churches on Maui, including Island Hope in Pa'ia and Kumalani Chapel in West Maui. They even sent an old Hope Hermosa member, Pat Hamman, to plant a church in Redmond, Washington. Today Hope Chapel Kihei numbers well over 1,000 people and reaches into Europe and Latin America with missionary zeal. It is the second largest congregation on Maui. Their greatest overseas accomplishment is a series of Christian schools among the *Moskito* Indians along the Rio Coco in Nicaragua. A Kihei member, Mike Bagby, visited the Honduras side of the river while the Moskitos were living there as exiles. They had been driven from their homeland by the Sandinista regime in Nicaragua. Mike soon returned to Honduras as a school planting missionary, flying back and forth from Florida in an ancient, single-engine airplane. His mission grew and soon crossed back over the river when the Moskitos returned home. Today, he and his crew train pastors and plant churches along with their other responsibilities.

Time's Up

Each time someone left with a team to start a church I'd feel a little sad. But I never connected those feelings with my own departure. One day it hit. Hard.

I was heading home one autumn day. My wife and I had our children stuffed in the jump seats of an old Porsche I'd restored. We had just come from surfing and sitting around in the sun at a friend's house on the beach. Afternoon shadows lengthened, and the Santa Ana winds blew warm. I plunged into depression: "I don't want to leave all this, I can't." I loved my friends and the California weather with its fall smells of smog and Coppertone. Even the Beach Boys on the car stereo seemed to cry out against our move. The whole scene represented everything I held dear, and it all seemed threatened by the move. I spent the next four months fighting depression.

The situation grew even more complicated. We received another wave of media attention. *Esquire* magazine ran a cover feature called "Men Who Walk on Water." What began as an essay on violence in surfing transformed into an eight-page saga of Christian surfers. The authors went looking for violence and found themselves being preached to by our young people. The Los Angeles newspapers picked up the story with full-page articles. Next, we hit the major television networks and a United Press International story showed up as far away as Toronto and Florida. I hadn't handled the first wave of publicity with all that much grace. This time was even worse. Besides the ego struggle, I had to deal with just how good we had it in California. I became more depressed.

The struggle seemed harder during those months. I didn't want to leave security, notoriety, good friends, and all that makes home lovely. I began to loathe the insecurity, obscurity and uncertainty of life in another state. Hawaii might be beautiful, but it was not home.

If control of your circumstances could be symbolized by the ring in Tolkien's books, I wanted to wear mine. Forget letting go. I prayed and even begged Got to remove the call to Hawaii. Instead, he took away the bad feelings.

I was surfing on a warm, winter morning when someone mentioned how the conditions reminded them of Hawaii. I poured out my bad feelings and selfish fears of uncertainty. My friends reminded me that I hadn't known the future in 1971 but had moved to South Bay with little more than my family and faith in the Lord. If he had been trustworthy then, wasn't he now?

I gave in. I let go of the ring, and the Holy Spirit gave me a whole new set of feelings. He also cracked the door just enough for us to see what might lay down the road.

Open Doors

I found out that an old friend, Dr. Robert Chang, had been named "honorary mayor of Kaneohe." We were looking for musicians to help make a splashy grand opening when Carole Kai, a well-known entertainer in Hawaii, joined our church in Hermosa. Her contacts solved our problem. KAIM Christian radio soon provided us an evening drive-time slot for our radio broadcast. We found ourselves sandwiched between some of the most popular speakers in their format. Thirty friends from the Hermosa Beach church moved with us to start the new venture. Some even moved to Oahu several months before Aaron and I could move our families. Through them, God gave us rich contacts with some of the local people who would become primary leaders in the new church.

Give God authority, and he will bless you beyond your dreams. Hold back and life is miserable. He's played this tug-of-war with folks throughout history. He isn't playing video games with our lives. He is trying to establish a chain of command toward real victory. Do you remember the Roman Centurion who said he was "under authority" before he asked Jesus to use his authority to heal his servant (Matthew 8:9)? Because he was under authority, he could recognize that Jesus' power came from being under the authority of God. We gain power by submitting to his authority. Letting go of the ring suggests we crawl off the throne and let him have complete authority over our lives. *Thy kingdom come, thy will be done* . . . in my own heart and life.

THE SOAP SALESMAN

You meet all kinds of people in church. There are surfers, housewives, bank operations people, carpenters and lots of aerospace types in the Hermosa Beach congregation. I've told you about bikers and small businessmen. Once a guy came confessing his dangerous and ill-fitted life of espionage. Then there was the soap salesman. The soap salesman is a story that's worth telling.

Now, this wasn't your average, run-of-the-mill soap salesman. The guy was well educated and had been around. Upon graduation from the University of Southern California, he traveled throughout Europe and Asia on the Hashish Trail. Later he opened a pharmacy in Kona, Hawaii. While handling legitimate drugs in the pharmacy, he bought and operated a marijuana farm in the mountains for more than two years. Then he discovered soap.

Our hero quit both drug businesses for a multilevel soap company. His was the kind that sold more dealerships than soap. It was more lucrative. He had three pyramids going with lots of people working for him when he visited Hope Chapel during our sojourn in the community center.

For his wife, church was a stab at saving their marriage. But for him, all that a church could offer was more business contacts. He lasted only two weeks. Not that he ran out of contacts. He ran into me. I was telling the church we were going to move to the bowling alley, though we'd lost it at an auction. "God gave us a wonderful plan to contact the new owner. . . ." The man thought I was nuts and he didn't want to get tainted. He'd sell soap elsewhere. Almost a year went by before I saw him again.

One afternoon he came home to an empty house. His wife had made off with his business partner. Everything was gone. She even took the phone. The wide-open front door mocked him as it waved in the breeze. Our friend says he would have done her violent harm if he had been able to find her. But finding her wasn't easy as he had hitchhiked home. She had even stolen his new Cadillac Seville off the street near where he worked that day.

By nightfall, the anger turned to pain. In that empty house he turned his life over to Jesus Christ. He had already noticed, with some consternation, that Hope Chapel now occupied the old bowling alley on top of the hill. The next morning, Zac Nazarian showed up in the church he would eventually pastor.

Two things stood out in the man. The first was devotion. He attended every service. I would even try to change my message a little bit between services just so he wouldn't get bored. Zac soaked up teaching like a dry sponge in water. The second characteristic was integrity. The man forgave his wife and gave her his home and everything they had owned. After the divorce, he humbly *asked* for an old Ford they had used as a second car. He "turned the other cheek," because the Lord said he should.

Let Go and Let Zac

As soon as I knew I was moving to Hawaii, I began praying for a successor. A smooth leadership transition was absolutely necessary. I ran in track and field events in college. One horrible memory is of losing a relay race. Someone dropped the baton during the hand off. That act symbolizes the way many churches change pastors. They fumble and stumble, losing precious time if not the race.

The Lord answered those prayers through Zac. Shortly after he was born again, he began pestering me about seminaries. I helped him find one. But I thought he attended simply to saturate himself with knowledge of God. I really didn't think he would become a pastor. But, he graduated and we quickly hired him part-time as a counselor. He was to fill in the rest of his time as a pharmacist. Not Zac. We caught up to him as his counseling schedule hit 55 hours a week. His new wife, Julie, worked as a flight attendant. They lived off her salary.

Zac gave himself to the ministry like no one I had ever known. Because counseling is hard on the emotions, we all teased him about being a masochist. We also restricted him to a 45-hour work week and gave him a raise.

Zac is a real learner. He quickly bought into our value system, something he didn't have time to grasp before he left for school. God forged a unique philosophy of ministry when he designed Hope Chapel. Too often, we've lost potential leaders to seminary education. Upon returning they can't reconcile their book knowledge with our practical position. Zac fitted himself into our position from start to finish. I attribute his adaptivity to the fact that he started and pastored a house church while attending seminary. His knowledge was tempered by experience.

Zac joined our staff about a year after my unsettling vision about Kaneohe. Sometime later I told him that I was leaving and thought that the Holy Spirit had told me that God wanted him to take my job. He was incredulous. He leaned over my desk, told me I was crazy and stomped out. I persisted and he hid out at home for two days, too sick to eat or sleep.

Up to this time I had only discussed the idea with one other man besides the Suzukis and my wife. His name was Tom

McCarthy. Tom filled the pulpit whenever I was away. The people loved him dearly. So dearly that our elders had an unwritten understanding that if I died or became disabled, Tom would take my place. Tom readily agreed that Zac was the person for the job. This was no light decision. Tom, an obstetrician, was thoroughly prepared to give up his practice to pastor the church (he eventually moved to Santa Rosa, planting a thriving Hope Chapel until his medical practice grew so large that he had to resign). Tom and I felt certain Zac was the guy. Zac was just as sure that we were nuts. When I told the church council my intentions to leave, they too agreed. Their was, "Who's going to take your place—Zac?"

God blessed the church in Hermosa Beach with Zac. More than that, he blessed me with Zac. This was a man after my own heart. Leaving the church in his capable hands made my departure much easier.

Throughout my last year in Hermosa, we modified our roles in anticipation of the future. I taught in the weekend services but made myself scarce during the week. It became handy for me to accept speaking engagements in seminars and conventions instead of showing up for work. This left Zac to administer our life at Hope Chapel during that year. He even launched three new churches and also taught in the Sunday evening service. Of course, it was a lame duck year for me. Attendance growth stalled as people adjusted to the change in leadership. The only area of growth during those 12 months was the Sunday evening attendance. Real overall growth only restarted after the Sunday I stepped aside and Zac moved into the pulpit. During my last six weeks in the church, I participated as a member, in the audience. Zac had become my pastor. Watching the resumption of growth bothered me, a little. The old ego took a bit of a bruising. On the other hand, I rejoice with all my heart. One of my disciples stepped into my shoes. We passed the baton without dropping it.

Stepping Aside

I once heard someone teach that a mark of God's "anointing" would be that no one could replace you. The exact opposite is true. Zac replaced me so well that I can be sure I was living in God's grace during my tenure in Hermosa Beach. Because I mentored him and the rest of the staff, their victories became my own. Their efforts are multiples of my own.

A fine team we make. In a sense, I never really left Hope Chapel Hermosa Beach. I continue as their missionary to Hawaii and other parts of the world. The New Testament term *apostle* means a person who is sent out from a particular location on a mission. The emphasis is on where they were sent *from*, not the place they were sent *to*. In other words, the heritage is the basis for the future ministry. Though my schedule won't let me travel there often, the church in Hermosa is still home base to me.

Pulling back from my job in California was painful. It would have been fun to keep every element of my job until the day we left. But, the church would have suffered. We hoped we could hand off the baton in a way other churches could model. No cold surprises. Our church knew I was leaving 18 months before the actual transition. They got to sample Zac, to get used to him. But this could only if I would stand aside, leaving him room to operate. Stepping aside was what any craftsman, scientist, or doctor would do to make room for their apprentice.

Speaking of doctors, you might be interested to know that I went to the dentist during my last week in California. Dr. Hiroshige had my mouth propped wide with all kinds of hardware while I was fitted for a crown. There was no chance for me to answer. Dr. Ken said, "Hey, I'm proud of you, Frodo, you really did it, you let go of the ring!"

Hope Chapel Hermosa Beach, California in its current state looks far better than when we found it.

This photo in the mid-1980's shows Ralph and Ruby with the staff team they left when moving to Hawaii. Bill Gross who planted in Cary, North Carolina is at the far right in the front row.

Good friends, fun cars and the California dream would soon be replaced by the action and excitement of planting a new congregation in Windward Oahu.

The Moores and Suzukis arriving in Honolulu in 1983. Jane Koki is at extreme left. Sonny Shimaoka is in the center.

Aaron Suzuki and Ralph Moore just after the move.

Hope Chapel Windward Oahu begins services at Kailua Beach Park.

Laying hands on Sonny and Sharon Shimaoka as they are sent out to plant Hope Chapel Kailua-Kona on the Big Island in 1984. Also pictured: Paul Hilker who planted Hope Chapel Farmers Branch, Texas and Zac Nazarian.

Mark and Laurie Souza, God's gift of music to Hope Chapels everywhere. Their worship songs soon set the tone for the unique worship sound of our churches.

John Bacigalupo, pastor of Hope Chapel Naha, Okinawa, our first church plant in Japan.

An early missions team departing for Japan. Yo Masui is second from the left, Corey Grinder third from left. Steve Fox is second from right and Kelly Moore, Ralph's daughter, is fourth from the right.

Craig and Kathy Englert at the dedication of the new church facility at Hope Chapel Kihei, Maui. The church now numbers well over one thousand people.

A visit with Randy and Janet Weir who planted Hope Chapel Ventura, California. The Weirs joined us the third Sunday on Manhattan Beach Boulevard.

Ralph, Homer Leong and Lisa Kai baptize Homer's wife, Lee. Hope Chapel baptisms always include family members and significant leaders in the life of the person being baptized.

Through the 1980s and early 1990s we held most baptisms at the beach.

Early photo of Hope Chapel Kaneohe staff. Back row: Ralph, John Honold, Aaron Suzuki, Stevie & Eric, Rick Petit. Middle row: Debra Tong, Carl Moore. Seated: Ruby, Stephanie Suzuki, Erin, Bonnie White, Kelly Moore, Suzie Beach.

Hope Chapel church planters reunion at an early 1990s Foursquare Pastor's Convention.

10

GIVE 'EM HEAVEN

Nothing's cooled off in Hermosa Beach. The church is healthy and touching thousands of people through its many outreaches.

Early in his ministry, Zac ended a service with a unique charge to the congregation. He said, "Too many people are giving each other hell all week. You go out there and give 'em heaven." The words caught fire in the hearts of the people. "Give 'em heaven!" became the rallying cry of a church bent on serving others.

NEW MINISTRIES

Giving away heaven's love is more like it. The congregation now boasts more than 100 active ministry teams operating alongside 85 MiniChurches. When I recently visited the church in Hermosa, the building was crawling with activity. Small groups of people huddled in every nook and cranny building ministry plans. Even the walls proclaimed care for people—I was overwhelmed by the hundreds of square feet of bulletin boards it takes to keep all the ministry groups in touch with each other:

There is a ministry to Khmer refugees that has helped develop churches in the Cambodian community in nearby Long Beach.

The ski club meets for fun and to do evangelism; both when the snow flies in the winter and behind big, fast water ski boats in the summer.

I picked up a piece of literature about a ministry group called "Breakaways." I discovered this was not the name for the prison ministry. It is a bicycle club that gets together for weekend fellowship rides, as well as serious competition.

As a ministry to prisoners in the California State Penitentiary at Chino and in the Terminal Island Federal Penitentiary, the church has begun an effort known as "Seventy times Seven." The name comes from Jesus' words in Matthew where he tells Peter that we should forgive someone "seventy times seven" and then some.

You can best understand the effect of the ministry through the words of inmate letters written as thanks for a weekend seminar the church held on the men's prison at Chino.

An inmate named Jonathan received Jesus during the seminar. He wrote, "That I happened to be here at Chino, I feel is beyond coincidence and I thank the Lord and Seventy times Seven for this blessing. I've been born again for one week now and already I can see a change . . ."

Another inmate named Kenneth said: " I think that the seminar finally gave the inmates here an alternative to organizations like the Mexican Mafia, etc. for survival in a maximum security prison and, ultimately, a way to stay out of prison once released."

You might remember to pray for the man who did not sign his letter. He wrote: "I know there's a jungle out there waiting for me to fall in the quicksand which I dread very much. I only wish I had found Jesus just like all of you have and I feel I am missing so very much because of all these past years Satan has turned me into a sick, hateful alcoholic. I want to change my life for God's sake and mine and I know I will!"

Seventy times Seven is indeed an exciting ministry opportunity and one directly commanded by the Lord in the gospels. The results go both ways. Besides the 41 inmates that opened their hearts to the Lord on that seminar weekend, several of the volunteers from the church wrote things like, "For the first time in my life, I really felt I was denying self and representing the love of Jesus. I knew I was where Jesus wanted me to be, presenting his LOVE to another human being. It was like a shock running through me."

Events like these are life changers for everyone involved.

The church continues to mature in other areas as well. There is now a well defined and effective team of volunteers organized for hospital visitation. This ministry is very important to the six or seven church members in local hospitals during any given week.

"Free to Choose" is a group of ministries offering help to anyone who wants freedom from life dominating sins. They minister to people suffering from drug addiction, alcoholism, suicidal drives, anger, and pornography. They even offer assistance to those struggling with overeating, anorexia, and other eating disorders. One foundational pillar under most of these groups is a 20-week course in self confrontation. The other is the assumption that helping others is the best way to help yourself. In their words, "Let's face it, most of us who suffer with compulsive behavior are very self-obsessed. Service helps release us from the nagging self-obsession which destroys our serenity. It is a way for us to give back to others some of what we have received. 'Give and it will be given unto you.'"

Another set of ministry groups is called "RISK." This stands for "Reaching Out in the Son's Kindness." These teams assist people experiencing difficulties due to crisis pregnancy, foster care, adoptions, hospice care, AIDS, cancer, bereavement, and divorce recovery.

The church doesn't shy away from social action either. They feed more than 100 hungry people on a weekly basis. Each Christmas, they minister to a couple hundred children of prisoners in the Los Angeles County Jails. The church holds a couple of used clothing drives each year to support Teen Challenge and operates several annual blood drives for the Red Cross.

Hope Academy, a well-organized home school, serves more than 200 children from 100 families with curriculum, sports and science classes.

OVERSEAS MISSIONS

Vision for ministry overseas is exploding. Teams have traveled to India, South Africa, Malawi, the Philippines, Romania, and Ecuador. There is ongoing work in South Africa where the church is committed to supporting the Foursquare missionaries. Jimi and Julaine Calhoun minister as Foursquare missionaries in Belize. Jimi has an interesting history. He enjoyed fame and made a lot of money as a member Sly and the Family Stone in the '70s. A couple of years after he turned to the Lord, he set it all aside asking for a job as a janitor in the Hermosa church so he could spend time hanging around the pastors learning the ministry. After several years of discipleship, he left Hermosa Beach and planted a Hope Chapel in Sherman Oaks, California. Now he's off to Belize. It's a pretty long way from the spotlights of huge rock concerts to this small nation on the north coast of South America. The church is a strong supporter of the Hindustan Bible Institute and Orphanage in Madras, India. This group under the leadership of Paul and John Gupta have trained several hundred Indian pastors. You can read their story in Dave Hunt's book, *God of the Untouchables,* available through Straight Street Resources. A ministry in Vietnam takes the form of a woman who carries in donated medical supplies along with God's love. In Yemen, bivocational missionaries share the gospel and make disciples while working at a secular job. Closer to home, people have made countless trips into Mexico to feed the poor and help with church construction. The church did much disaster relief in both Honduras and Nicaragua in the wake of Hurricane Mitch.

One interesting move for Zac and the people in Hermosa is their annual presentation of the play, "Heaven's Gate & Hell's Flames." This drama has the devil out, interacting with the audience, menacing people in their seats. Pretty unsophisticated stuff for a California beachside community. Zac says it is definitely not his style. The staff refused to offer it when first presented with the idea. They finally agreed to try it after hearing of its effectiveness as a tool for evangelism. Since the church began their presentation, more than 8,000 people have

144 / RALPH MOORE

accepted Christ in three years. The results are startling. People actually run to the front of the auditorium, crashing to their knees in humility and repentance toward God. The current goal is for 5,000 people to receive Christ in one season of nine showings.

PLANTING CHURCHES

What excites me most is that the leadership of Hope Chapel in Hermosa has continued with the vision to plant churches. Since I left Hermosa, successful new congregations have sprung up in many cities around the west.

Soon after I moved to Hawaii, Randy Sanford, planted a Hope Chapel in Colorado. Bob Mallord used to deal cocaine. Now he pastors Hope Chapel in Venice, California. Gary Sinardi pioneered our first church in Salt Lake City, Utah. Dale Yancy and Jeff Fischer started a church with a group of people Jeff led to the Lord in Northridge, California. Steve Mullen began a counseling center and built a church from that base in Sandy, Utah. Mark Keever launched Hope Chapel Gateway in Torrance, California. There is another strong ministry nearby. Don Shoji began Hope Chapel in the Holiday Inn in Torrance. Bill Gross, a former worship leader, began Hope Chapel Redondo Beach. Bill later moved to Cary, North Carolina, where he planted a congregation of 500 people. Bill Gross has become a strong leader within the Foursquare Church. His role is strategizing with and launching church planters in the southeastern United States.

Long after I left Hermosa the church continues with a strong trail of church planters and pastors. They include: Rick Fallo in

Gardena, Henry Kaney in Harbor City, and Howard Mayeda in San Pedro. Dan Brown planted Hope Chapel San Pedro, Barry Felis planted in Torrance. George Magdaleny is in Hawthorne, Scott Dotanville in Colorado Springs. Jose Peres planted Hispanic congregations in Hawthorne and Hermosa Beach. Sergio and Josie Samonet pastor a mobile congregation that moves about. They follow horse-trainers as they circle among the Southern California race tracks. Finally, Chris Cannon recently left Hope Hermosa to assume the pastorate of a tiny congregation near King Harbor in Redondo Beach. Renamed *King's Harbor Fellowship,* the church immediately exploded to 500 members and has trouble finding large enough quarters for its continued growth.

HOPE CHAPEL MASTER'S

Follow-up support to the daughter churches became an immediate difficulty when I left for Hawaii. Zac could oversee those pastors who left under his ministry, but he could hardly be expected to input to the lives of men who began pastoring before he got saved. Most of them looked to him for leadership, but he felt inadequate. Zac is a humble man. He once told me that I was like a spiritual father to them while he was merely a stepfather.

The problem is now well in hand with the development of something called "Hope Chapel Master's Program." Once a month, Zac brings in a highly-qualified instructor to sharpen the skills of our pastors. Tapes of the sessions are mailed to those outside of driving distance. This plan has proven an invaluable supplementary education, addressing such issues as church finance, the pastor's home life, stress avoidance, discipline and ethics.

The mother church is not suffering from the birthing process. Each week large numbers of people express new-found faith in the Lord through the prayer time at the end of the services. The people of Hope Chapel do a fantastic job sharing Jesus' love with their friends and relatives. Their efforts pay off in commitments to the Kingdom of God. Every six weeks, more than 100 people proclaim their faith by getting baptized in the "big hot tub" in the auditorium.

TRAINING

We should always remember that a church is people, never a building.

The New Testament says we are like bricks or "living stones" built into a spiritual temple for the Lord. If we are the stones, then love and commitment are the mortar. The church exists to train its members for acts of ministry to one another and the world.

The Hermosa church is doing a great job with this training process. Their success is evidenced by the numbers we looked at earlier. But let me tell you some of the exciting things they are doing in order to train others.

They now have three levels of "Roots" training for new Christians. Nine hundred people went through those classes in 1991.

The church now offers a series of one-day seminars for aspiring MiniChurch pastors. MiniChurch pastors are getting much more hands-on training as they care for their own people.

The church is built around the MiniChurch concept. This allows for a much larger ministry and pastoral care team, as well as the training opportunity that produces churches in other localities. The great exodus to lower-cost housing in Orange and San Diego counties brought an attrition of MiniChurch pastors, but many new people are rising up to take their place.

The Hope Chapel Ministries Institute enrolled 825 people in classes during 1991, and many of those are MiniChurch pastors hoping to go on and plant a new church in the future.

The entire church recently read through the Daily Bible together for the second year in a row. People are interested in the Scriptures for the power they give to live a godly life. These people are committed to bring light into their world.

A NEW LEADER FOR A NEW DAY

It's funny how the Lord has to move his people around to accomplish his purposes.

The years have proven an old theory of mine. I don't believe any leader is capable of everything, and I do believe God raises up different people for different times.

Roughly translated, that means that God had me in Hermosa Beach for the first stage in the life of that congregation. He anointed Zac Nazarian to take them through the second major growth period of their life as an assembly.

God works today much like he did in ancient Israel. Moses brought the nation out of bondage in Egypt, but it was Joshua who led them to occupy Palestine. Not too much later, it was David who brought them respectability and set the tone for the reign of Jesus as Messiah.

The congregation at Hermosa Beach is where they are today only because God sent me to another place and brought them his man for this hour. I say that with no lack of self-confidence. I simply believe that God called me as a pioneer and that he equipped Zac as an organizer and developer. Neither of us would be much good in the other's role.

Zac almost immediately led the congregation into a building program. The idea was so visionary that I thought it a mistake when I first heard about it. But after a couple of hours and several cups of coffee, I was convinced he was hearing God. The need to enlarge the facility was obvious by the overcrowding at every service.

BUYING LUCKY MARKET

One day, a few years after leaving, I called Hope Hermosa to get some information. I discovered that the church had just put in an offer to buy the supermarket next door. The offer was invited by the company that owned the market, so no one is just dreaming. The congregation now owns that property. They bought it for a couple of million dollars from an insurance company. We are talking about a supermarket with acres of parking and a spectacular view of the Pacific Ocean. The reason for the wonderful price is that the property is under a lease to Lucky (recently purchased by Albertsons) until the year 2007.

In February 1992, Zac sent a letter to the entire church asking the members to stop sending money to the building fund. The bowling alley-turned-church, the supermarket for future development, and three houses for a parking lot are all debt-free. Nearly $1.5 million sits in the bank, waiting to transform the market into a church auditorium. There is simply no need for more money. This reminds me of Moses asking the people to stop giving to the tabernacle construction in Exodus 35 and 36. When God's people learn the secret of faithful tithing, two things happen. First, their church is strengthened to the point where there can be less reliance on building funds and special offerings. There will be enough money so the church can go forward in strength (Malachi 3:10). The second blessing is that of God's financial grace in the lives of his people. As they give generously, he promises to provide enough to meet their needs, the church's needs through them, *and* to add surplus to their lives so they can become aggressively generous (2 Corinthians 9:10-11). Because the people in Hermosa learned that lesson early on, they have a strong financial track record in the church, its buildings and ministries, as well as in their personal lives.

The great need, of course, is to buy out the lease and remodel the market into badly-needed church facilities. Only the Lord knows when that will happen. In the meantime, I'm proud of Zac and company for having the integrity to turn away funds. They are helping restore credibility that Christianity has lost in the past few years.

A PROVEN MINISTRY

Hope Hermosa has proven itself. Too often we hear of churches in trouble after a long-tenured senior pastor leaves. This congregation has only grown in grace and in vision.

He won't own up to it, but a lot of that has to do with a man named Zac Nazarian. It took three years before he admitted he even felt like the pastor. It is quite obvious to the rest of us that

God chose the right man and that the man walks in serious obedience to his master. We all win for it!

Since I left in 1983, Hope Hermosa hasn't missed a beat. The original vision that God gave a bunch of young hippies back in 1971 continues to bear fruit well into the '90s. We can only expect that kind of fruit where people sincerely walk in faith and abide in Christ.

11

CHURCH ON THE BEACH

Church on the beach! Sounds like fun, *huh?* Let me tell you how much fun it really was. I know you'll have a great laugh.

For nearly a year before moving to Hawaii we negotiated for a place to meet for church. Just before we moved, those negotiations fell through. Our hopes crashed with them. Our family had moved out of our home. I had surrendered my job. We'd just spent three weeks living out of suitcases while I taught in summer camps. Everything we owned was in mid-ocean somewhere between Los Angeles and Honolulu when the call came. The building deal was off. We would have no place to hold services. Without a meeting place a congregation is hard pressed to exist. Without meeting space, a pastor has no job. The entire plan was in jeopardy and those of us in leadership were pretty confused.

DID WE MISREAD GOD?

My first reaction was anger, and then fear, that feeling of nausea that comes when things escape your control. You've had those feelings a few times, yourself. Amplify them by the thought, "I might not have really heard God in the first place." Those feelings were not disruptive. They were terrifying. I was anything but a model of faith.

The building deal completely died. And it wasn't about to resurrect. Aaron Suzuki and I immediately flew to Oahu to round up other possibilities. One church said they might rent to us on Sunday evenings. They soon changed their mind. Worse yet, they wrote us a rather nasty letter. They warned us to stay on the mainland. In their eyes, Hawaii had its fill of evangelicals. We got their letter an hour before we and our families boarded the plane for Honolulu. If that was a lousy send-off, the reception was no prettier.

A Wet Reception

We arrived to meet a hurricane warning and more rain than I had seen in the entire previous year. To make matters gloomier, I had rented a house in one of the rainiest areas of our island. Our shoes grew green mold just sitting in the closets.

Difficult Neighbors

The rain was bad and the neighbors grievous. Across the street lived two people with too much time on their hands. They kept themselves busy policing the neighborhood. They called the cops because they thought it was illegal to park a moving truck at the side of the road. Of course it was not, but they caused the hassle they intended.

They phoned the police again when my friend parked his rental car in front of my house overnight. That, too, is legal.

These lovely people struck gold when they complained about the Bible studies in our living room. The uniformed police were called twice, and a building inspector once. The new problem was too many cars parked in front of one house. The harassment finally got to us and we moved the study. I thank the Lord that I was also able to move my family after just two months of those "neighborly" people.

On the Beach

So much for the home front. Our new church began as a large Bible study which we split into three MiniChurches. These groups gathered for three weeks before we held our first Sunday gathering. Weekend services began with 64 people meeting Sunday mornings at the beach. We met under a hau tree in Kailua Beach Park. With no permit, we worried constantly about disruption from the authorities. We even faced the congregation away from the parking lot so people wouldn't see a possible approaching police officer. We figured that I could dismiss the service in an orderly manner while Aaron and our new friend Sonny Shimaoka stalled the officer.

Of course, we really had no major problems with the police. The previous difficulties in the neighborhood weren't the fault of the police. They were always kind and even apologized for being forced to respond to the calls.

You should have seen our setup! The people piled beach chairs and boogie boards everywhere. They brought tons of food, and ice chests abounded. It looked more like a company picnic than a church meeting. It had to. That was our disguise.

This church on the beach stuff may sound humorous. But it wasn't funny to us. Satan did his best to keep us from a legitimate meeting place. We found no pleasure in our circumstances at the time.

Heavenly Showers

The last week on the beach it rained, and I was actually happy it did. Our people had quickly grown attached to our beautiful, rent-free location. Kailua has repeatedly been voted "The World's Most Beautiful Beach." The park is stunning, but would have prevented growth and any sense of real order in our meetings. During our last week there, we rented a building eight miles away for our first sheltered worship location. The long drive and confinement of a building made the beach look better than ever. The rain on our final beach day helped people feel thankful for the anticipated move.

WORSHIPING UNDER ROOF(S)

The new location was a former restaurant at He'eia State Park. The park had a long history as a private park. Some old-timers may remember it as Ulu Mau Village.

A really great guy named Doug Mersberg managed the place. His governing board went to great lengths to convince the park system that it was legal to rent to a church. We will be forever grateful to those people, as well as a man named Hugh Conser. Hugh was a member of another church. He was also a real estate developer. He felt called to help us. Hugh spent three weeks combing Windward Oahu for rentable space. It was he who worked up the relationship with He'eia State Park. Hugh was a one-man welcome wagon sent from God.

We met at He'eia from October 1983 through April 1984 when we moved to Kapunahala Elementary School. Nice things happened at Kapunahala. The church immediately grew to more than 400 people. We had more space, and we filled it. I also gained a wonderful friend in Jimmy Yoshimori, the principal. Jimmy introduced me to many people in the community. It was through his friendship that I finally stopped feeling like such an outsider to life in my community.

We celebrated our first church birthday with a *luau,* a Hawaiian-style love feast. Five hundred people showed up at our anniversary service. We had exceeded our five-year goal of 450. There had never before been a large Protestant church in Windward Oahu. Kaneohe is a small town. The entire community consists of just over 40,000 people. All our friends thought we were crazy to pray for "such a big church in just five years." It turned out that we had sold the Lord short on his ability to build his church. We had also failed to grasp the great spiritual hunger in the community.

JUST THE RIGHT PEOPLE

The first year was filled with surprises. The best were people who came to figure significantly in the ministry team. I had prayed for a Christian to build a surf shop as a base for evangelizing young people. I knew what an influence good surfers have on the younger kids around them. The week we started church in Hawaii, Straight Up Surfboards opened for business. We didn't realize it at the time, but the guys who started the company were part of our church. For many years their shop was a hot spot for evangelism. It produced many strong, young leaders.

Even the building where we leased office space proved a trail head to blessing. We discovered an architect's office in the building that would let us use their photocopy machine at a reasonable rate. The office manager was a young woman named Debra Tong; within a year she joined our fellowship and became our office manager. For nearly 10 years, Debbie was my secretary. She currently overseas production and marketing for our Straight Street Resource Center. We thank God for that copy machine.

One day, in the elevator, I met a man who asked if we did marriage counseling. I told him we did, and invited him to church. He came to church with his wife and they gave their hearts to the Lord. Their marriage got better due to mass infusions of God's word. I don't know if they ever did make it in for the counseling. Rob and Debbie McWilliams joined my MiniChurch and moved on to help start Hope Chapel Leeward in Pearl City. Later, Rob took on the men's ministries in our church. He then joined our pastoral team as a full-time member. Rob's latest responsibility was construction of our new worship facility. You never know who you are going to meet in an elevator.

By our third anniversary we moved to Benjamin Parker Elementary School off Kamehameha Highway in Kaneohe. The move gave us larger facilities and the ability to park more cars. Ben Parker School is really the *de facto* community center for Kaneohe. We feel very fortunate that the faculty was willing to share their building with us on weekends. Without their patience we would have really faced a huge problem. It is very difficult for a congregation of our size to fit under a tree.

The church grew to about 1,600 in average weekly attendance during the Ben Parker years. We expanded to 115 MiniChurches spread over the island from Hawaii Kai to Mililani to Makakilo. The MiniChurches are the backbone of our congregation as they were in California. The maturing leaders carry an ever-growing load of ministry as they introduce the practicalities of the word of God into people's lives.

WAS IT WORTH IT?

During the first four years in Hawaii, people wearied me with the same question: "Was it worth it?" The answer will never change: "Of course it was worth it!" Obedience to God is always worth it. You cannot lose your life, by seeking to do so for his sake. You only lose by trying to cling to it.

Usually the questioner is wondering if Hawaii is really a nice place to live and is not so concerned with the element of obedience. Hawaii is a lovely place to live, but so was California. The only real issue is that of walking in obedience to the Spirit. No matter how good or bad the physical surroundings, the only paradise this world offers is a walk in the Spirit. In 1983 my family and a few good friends moved nearly 3,000 miles. We set up housekeeping in a place that was new and foreign to us. We all felt a little like Abraham as we packed our bags and headed for a land the Lord would show us. It was a costly and painful change but very worthwhile.

A Tale of Two Cities

Besides all the great stories of new friends and warm experiences, there are tangible spiritual results. The Kingdom of

God has grown. Because we moved to Hawaii, a second "church-planting church" was born. Hope Hermosa continued to plant churches aggressively. We matched them in enthusiasm. We like to think of them as the Jerusalem church and of ourselves as the congregation in Antioch. Antioch was born of Jerusalem and both churches birthed a host of others (Acts 11:19-24).

Lots of New Churches

We began Hope Chapel Windward (now Hope Chapel Kaneohe) in September 1983. Aikahi Christian Fellowship got off the ground with our help five months later. Pastor Mike Hubbard lived in the islands working with another ministry. God put it in his heart to plant a church, but he lacked financial backing and commitment of his friends. Through our friendship, the Lord brought the church to birth. Several people who were attending our fellowship joined with Mike and his wife Joy in their new venture.

Among those who joined them were Paul and Susan Hilker who came to Hawaii with us from Hermosa Beach. The Hilkers assisted Mike during the early days in Aikahi and then moved on to Texas. They planted Hope Chapel Foursquare Church in Carrollton, a suburb of Dallas. By helping us, and then Mike, they received the education and the impetus for starting that church.

A year after we started, our first MiniChurch pastor and worship leader, Sonny Shimaoka, and his wife, Sharon, assumed the pastorate of a church in Kona on the Big Island. The church had lost their pastors and shrunk to a membership of only seven people. Sonny built it into a thriving congregation and became a leader in his new community.

A year after Sonny started, a mutual friend of ours and a neighbor to the Shimaokas, Greg Kirschmann and his wife, Sandy, started Keahou (now Holualoa) Chapel in Kona. While Sonny ministers to a large family of local folks, Greg started with transplanted mainlanders. The two pastors are great friends, and Kona will never be the same because of them.

Back on Oahu, two other exciting new churches grew out of Hope Chapel Windward while those guys were building on the Big Island. Chuck and Kathy planted a congregation in Pearl City High School. The church eventually moved and became Hope Chapel Waipahu. In the process, they equipped Rob McWilliams for pastoral ministry. We hired him shortly afterwards.

In Waikiki, Jack and Marie Nordgren pastor a Hope Chapel in a local community center. They reach out to the residents who live in the shadow of tourist hotels, with the constant hustle and bustle of the resort world around them. Jack, a former street evangelist and follow-up man for the Waikiki Beach Chaplaincy, is particularly suited to that mission field.

The first Hope Chapel church plant in Japan was born of our move to Hawaii. John Bacigalupo received Christ in Okinawa in a spectacular, though disconcerting, manner. A dyslexic, he had no access to God through his word and had not found him in the very traditional church of his youth. His marriage went sour. Life in the Marine Corps was unfulfilling. He found no solace in drugs. Minutes away from suicide at the barrel of his service revolver, John heard God tell him to read the Bible. John argued that he could not. He was still dyslexic. God persevered. John argued back and forth for several minutes with what seemed like an audible voice.

In anger, he picked up the Bible to prove his point. To his amazement, he could read! Most appropriately, he fell on his knees and surrendered his life to Jesus. John still cannot write without help from his wife, but he has graduated from college.

He and his wife, Tosh, ran our Christian education program for a year. They then moved back to Okinawa where John served his last assignment as a sergeant in the United States Marine Corps. Hope Chapel Naha now numbers nearly a hundred people. God provided stability in the form of a lovely rented church building. However, they now own land and are in the process of constructing a new church facility.

The hundreds of people who populate these congregations walk in fellowship with each other and the Lord because a few people trusted God and let go of their own personal security.

These new churches place a high value on personal evangelism, so they further the cause of Christ more rapidly and obey the Great Commission at a faster pace. Thus, the faster we plant new churches, the better chance we have of introducing large numbers of people to Jesus. This is true, even if those churches are small in their beginnings.

Consider if we had never left California. Hope Chapel in Hermosa Beach would probably have grown to roughly the same size it is now. The church would have presumably commissioned the same number of pastors under my leadership as it has under Zac. We would enjoy all the same successes. But Hawaii, Japan, and several other places would remain untouched because the church in Kaneohe wouldn't exist. Because we moved to Hawaii, Zac stepped up to the plate. Our two congregations, together, have twice the impact. Also, by plowing new ground in Hawaii and Asia, we stretched the vision for all the churches in the Hope Chapel network. The results that come from obedience are exciting when you take time to consider them.

Counting the Costs

Not only did my family and the Suzukis trust God in coming here, but so did a whole congregation of people on the mainland. They funded us, they prayed faithfully, they even gave up their pastors and friends.

There were several costs to the venture that we did not anticipate. Communication between daughter churches on the mainland broke down for a while. I was too busy to look after the congregations we had planted while I pastored in Hermosa. Zac felt he had little to offer men who pastored for more years than he was a Christian. However, those difficulties actually strengthened our relationship with our denomination. Our daughter churches were forced to build tighter relationships with the rest of the Foursquare family.

Another cost came from distortion of our vision. A few people could not understand why a pastor would leave a large, happy church. They believed that we were all mad at each other. Their suggestions really hurt.

The greatest cost was homesickness. It was more painful than I ever imagined. We found ourselves missing people we knew well, but not well enough for them to come visit. Cafes and favorite walks by the beach crept into my dreams. Those were haunting days.

Our children had to adjust to new schools and new friends. Ruby and I anguished as they struggled with a new culture. But

God was good to them throughout the process. Both Carl and Kelly made wonderful friends and did well in school. A side bonus was their involvement in the ministry. Because the church was new, they found opportunity to serve that they would have missed by staying in California. It paid off. Today, Carl and his wife, Kanani, serve as successful youth pastors in Huntington Beach, California. Kelly recently married Travis White. Anticipating missionary work, the two of them are deeply involved in discipleship training at churches in Torrance and Redondo Beach.

TRUE PARADISE

Hawaii isn't paradise any more than California or any other beautiful location. During the hard times I used to question whether I really heard from God at the beginning of this venture. I've had to realize that every life contains struggles that make it interesting, as well as painful. Had we remained in Hermosa, we would have faced battles similar to those we found in Hawaii. We followed God and inherited a mixed bag of victory and uncertainty. We also got to participate in his victories. There are no paradises, no primrose lanes in this world, only the joy of obedience. The move was, and is, well worth it!

12

BUILDING BRIDGES

Did you ever meet a "mighty man?" The Old Testament describes them as hooligans, debtors and rebels. These were the men who joined David in the Cave of Adullum (1 Samuel 22:1-2). Under David's leadership, they became men of God. Their exploits were an obvious expression of God's supernatural power in people lined up with his purpose (2 Samuel 23:8-39 KJV). They lost out in their first turn at life. Under David, God gave them a second chance. Churches often become "societies of the self-righteous." I want our church to function as a team of second chances.

Jesus went into the world and chose some apparent losers. He called them to himself and forged a team that today comprises nearly one-third of the population of the planet. It would probably be larger if we remembered that he sent us to the lost and dying, the poor and broken rather than the rich and well put together.

The Christian church exists to offer second chances. This is true at conversion. God promises to love us in spite of our sin and failure. But what about the leadership team? It is often the misfit who is capable of the greatest creativity and is motivated to the greatest love. Jesus said that he who was the most forgiven would love the most. Some are forgiven much at the point of conversion. Others find the need for forgiveness after they launch themselves into the ministry.

FIRED TWICE AND ALWAYS FIRED UP

A good example is Jeff MacKay. Today, he ministers in Osaka, Japan. Before planting the congregation in Japan, Jeff planted Hope Chapel Mililani, Hawaii. Begun with a handful of high school students, the church now numbers more than 500 people. Before Mililani, he worked for me . . . several times. I had to fire him twice.

I met Jeff back in Hermosa Beach. He worked his way through LIFE Bible College by running our church printing press. He didn't show a lot of promise from the outside. Blond surfer hair falling in his face, wire-rimmed glasses sliding down his nose, and a case of mild dyslexia didn't pose him as "most likely to succeed."

Jeff is quite artistic. And like many artists, he wasn't terribly organized. The short story: I fired him from our print shop for sloppy work. That was shortly before I moved to Hawaii. He surprised me by asking if he could come help us start the new church. No bitterness. Jeff knew he needed to tighten up on the work front. Also, having just graduated, he wanted to pursue the pastorate. The plan was for him to obtain secular employment and work in the church as a volunteer. You guessed it. He got a job in a print shop.

Jeff quickly started a junior high Bible study. It immediately grew to more than 40 students. Young people grew in the Lord, but their parents weren't too pleased with Jeff. "Mister Disorganization" had a problem with schedules and curfews. A bad situation exploded one Saturday afternoon. Seems he took a bunch of kids hiking over a broken suspension bridge 75 feet above a deep and dangerous gulch. When the parents heard about it, I had to remove him from the youth group. In other words, he got fired again.

Jeff's response? He started a high school group. He figured those parents wouldn't stress out so much if their kids stayed out late. From my point of view, Jeff MacKay had become an unstoppable force. Nothing deterred him from the ministry. Within a couple of months there were more than 70 high schoolers attending the Bible study groups he started! This persevering young man soon found employment as our full-time high school pastor.

Jeff eternally overspent his budget. We often had to bail him out of trouble with parents. But he always learned from the inevitable discipline. Besides, effective ministry oozed from him. Kids got saved and lives changed! A natural evangelist, Jeff told people about the Lord everywhere he went, even in Japan, before he could speak Japanese. He would pantomime, draw pictures, or use a dictionary. Jeff always did whatever it took to introduce people to the Lord. Jeff went beyond receiving forgiveness to become the picture of effectiveness. My relationship with Jeff MacKay reminds me of Abraham Lincoln and Ulysses S. Grant. Lincoln responded to criticism for depending on Grant, a known alcoholic. He told critics, "I need Grant, the man will fight." His other generals got good marks for deportment. But they wouldn't do the single thing most required for battlefield success. Jeff MacKay may have been disorganized and youthfully immature, but he sure was successful.

A Church Is Born

One day he shared the Lord with a high school girl from Mililani after surfing. She spread the word to her friends, and they soon started a Bible study. Someone from another Hope Chapel taught the study for a while but felt ill-prepared to handle their ballooning numbers. It soon became apparent that a church was trying to be born. Those kids recruited Jeff and Hope Chapel Mililani came into the world. The odd thing about its birth is that I tried to stop it. I didn't think Jeff was ready. I also wanted him to stay around and "pay back" for all the mentoring we had put into him. If I had prevailed that day, we would be without one large church in the family and short one very successful missionary to Japan.

Mentor as "Protector"

The most powerful management book of the 1980s was Tom Peters' *In Search of Excellence*. It is a manual for successful business and service organizations. I've read it several times. Each time I do, I'm struck with Peter's concept of a mentor or "champion." Tom Peters would see the apostle Paul as more than a teacher to Timothy or Silas. *In Search of Excellence* describes the need for the older man to train, role model, and *protect* the younger leader. Part of equipping God's people to do his work includes protecting them while they make their mistakes.

This is a great and rewarding part of my job as pastor and equipper. I am constantly challenged to work with failure in those I train. Everyone who succeeds powerfully usually fails badly at one time or another. Success is reserved for risk-takers —so is failure.

Success and Failure

The *difference* between success and failure is twofold. Success requires (A) Willingness to learn from mistakes. (B) Getting lots of chances to swing the bat. During his baseball career, Reggie Jackson struck out more times than any batter in history. He also broke just about every batting record around. You have to swing at an enormous number of pitches to hit lots of home runs. In ministry, you must take chances with people or you never produce great leaders.

Reggie Jackson's managers and coaches put up with the strikeouts in order to win pennants. I had to learn this where Jeff MacKay was concerned. The lesson was for me, not him. If I try to protect my own reputation (hang on to that ring of control), I will miss out on men like Jeff. I wish every pastor and church board could learn the tolerance and patience Jeff taught us. Too often bright young leaders get cast aside by mature men and women who insist on perfection instead of results.

There were plenty of times that I wanted to give up on Jeff. I worried about what others might think of me or of the church due to his behavior. Today, I am proud of our reputation due to Jeff's great accomplishments. If my fears had won, our ministry would certainly be smaller. Jesus spoke of this when he said you must lay down your life (including reputation) for his sake if you really want to find it. He also said that if you try to hold on to your life, you will lose it (Matthew 16:24-28). The challenge for me continues: "Can I see people through the Lord's eyes? Will I cooperate with his plan for them? Or will I worry about safely getting through life with a limited amount of trouble?"

HARD HEADS

One my greatest challenges in laid-back Hawaii is cultural. It involves raising local leadership. I have been accused of being racially prejudiced against Caucasians or *haoles* because our church focuses so heavily on local people. But I recognize a need to equip the saints that live here to do God's work. Our goal is to serve the entire populace, not just folks who move from the mainland. To accomplish this task, we need to equip local leadership. Sometimes easier said than done.

To an outsider, local males *seem* to just "hang loose" while the mainland *haole* is raring to go. Actually, the local guy may be just a little more cautious than his mainland counterpart. Local culture includes the notion of "shame." Better not to try than to risk shaming yourself and your friends. Throw in a mix of Asian fears about pride, and leadership recruitment becomes a daunting task. Mainlanders volunteer. Locals usually wait to be asked. Careful recruitment keeps our team reflective of our entire community.

Driven by Success

The opposite extreme is the local person who is *driven* by success. Two such people are John Honold and Corey Grinder. Both were, and are, very good at any thing they do. Both were deeply involved in our church. They are both Japanese-Caucasian by descent. They are each highly competitive. One more similarity—they didn't use to like each other. John came to us while we still worshiped on the beach. Corey arrived three years later. We were thrilled with both of them until we discovered they had been rivals since they were in high school. Neither could rid his mind of the other. They played football against each other. They competed for modeling jobs at the same department store. They even dated the same girls. Now they worked (and bickered) on the same church staff.

John was our first singles pastor and later worked wonders as high school pastor. Corey followed John in singles and became our first missions director. John went on to plant (thousand-member) Hope Chapel Kapolei. He's planted churches in Hawaii and in Okinawa. Corey is a very successful missionary pastor in Hope Chapel Tokorozawa, Japan. He is also the Tokyo area supervisor for churches in the Foursquare denomination.

Knocking Heads

For several years the two of them would knock heads whenever possible. The undercurrent affected everything from staff meetings to worship events. Their animosity was like a malignancy under chemotherapy. It would shrink under active discipline, only to quickly grow back. I anguished over their attitudes but felt they were worthy of patience and personal investment. Tough and tenacious, these men both held wonderful potential. They excelled at life by hurling themselves headlong at any obstacle in their way. Their strong opinions and tendency to "grab for the ring" had purchased bittersweet "success" in the world. But it only tainted their potential before the Lord.

One day I spent four hours with the two of them in a coffee shop. It was an attempt to catalyze their conversation. I insisted they "have it out" and forsake their particular form of insanity. I'm not sure the meeting did any good. I do know they solved their problems and became great friends. They preach in each other's churches and stay in each other's homes. I think they did it of their own choosing and that it had something to do with maturity. Strong ministry gifts aside, these guys needed time to grow up. My role was simply to take a little heat from others while giving these hard heads time to soften.

BRIDGING TO JAPAN

In 1985 we sent four young men to Japan for a summer outreach. Two of them were Jeff MacKay and Corey Grinder. They led one young boy to the Lord. He brought along 14 of his friends. Within six months those boys brought enough excitement home that the total number of new people in the church was 45. Many of their parents became Christians. I wish the story ended with growth. But it does not. Six months later, only the first boy and his father were walking with the Lord. The boy eventually fell away.

These boys belonged to a Japanese version of a street gang. When the first of them ran away from home, he came to the church where my friends were staying, because his dad knew the pastor. That dad is the only person left out of what should have grown into a time of revival.

You have to ask, "Why did the others fall away?"

Church Culture *vs* Relationship

It seems that the culture of that church was too isolated from the culture of non-Christian Japanese people. Americans have a heavy influence upon church songs and traditions in Japan. That influence often renders the church too "un-Japanese" for most people to feel comfortable.

Only the man who already knew the pastor remained with the church. He was the only person with a built-in "bridge" into the life of that congregation. That bridge allowed him to overcome the "foreignness" of the church environment. He stuck with it long enough to learn the necessary vocabulary, music tastes and behavior code that would allow him to fully participate.

Shared Values and Tastes

Studies show that people like to worship God in the presence of those they know and trust. They also prefer to worship with people sharing tastes similar to their own.

The reason some churches grow, while others do not, is their ability to present faith in friendly and familiar terms. People respond to love and they respond to familiar styles of music, dress, communication, and even architecture. In our own church, 87 percent of the people came through the invitation of a friend. Sixty-five percent of our people got saved through the ministry of someone *in our own* church. This suggests that we are "packaging" the gospel in terms familiar with our generation and culture.

The burden to *adapt* is on the teacher rather than on the learner. Paul circumcised Timothy in order to maintain an audience with Jewish people he targeted (Acts 16:1-3). His goal was to adapt to the cultural demands of his audience. In the same way, I had to adapt to reach hippies back in California. Our style changed again when those hippies turned to yuppies. My whole approach to life changed drastically when I moved to Hawaii. I had to adapt in order to understand and communicate with the people I wanted to reach.

Lately, I've learned to speak a little Japanese. Along with it I'm learning some surprising things about Japanese people. Japan is changing rapidly. Every newspaper you read has at least one article about social change in that country. The change upsets many people, but it opens new doors for the gospel.

A New Generation

For a while younger people in Japan were often called *Shinjinrui*. The term ties together the Japanese written characters for three separate words: new, man, and dragon. New-man-dragon. The suggestion is of a generation out of control. They have vastly different views from their parents on most issues. As the generation gap became more pronounced, Shinjinrui was replaced with terms like "monster" and "Martian." "They are so different that they must come from outer space." With these words, Japanese elders bemoan loss of control over their young.

Rapid change is a relatively new phenomenon in Japan. For generations, people simply adopted the values and traditions of their elders. The Japanese national proverb is, "The nail that stands up will be driven down." It means that you don't dare stand out in a crowd. The overwhelming need to conform defined this society for many generations. Young kids clad in the fashion of the month continually "drive down" this ancient proverb and the society it once defined.

Economic shock and a new position in the world of power and politics drastically affect street-level values. Young people are more likely to identify with an Irish rock group than with the music and poetry of Japan. Clothing styles are European. Attempting to monitor California fads, every Japanese car manufacturer has a design studio in Los Angeles. There was a period when young Japanese imitated African-American athletes and entertainers. Nothing new, the whole world imitates worthy heroes. But the Japanese would go to extremes. Many would paint their faces black and wear clothes replicating a publicity photo of their latest idol. Without hope of home ownership, young Japanese spend conspicuously on cars, clothes, and entertainment. Unlike any other postwar generation they desire free time above job promotion or security. They also pack along a new set of social problems. Violent crime and scandals over cheating on school admission tests outrage the whole country. Teenage prostitution, involving otherwise respectable young girls, is a growing problem.

Recent investment banking scandals brought upheaval to a staid economic system. New revelations have shown *yakuza* (Japanese mafia) tentacles firmly attached to legitimate business and government leaders. The price tag for decades of prosperity has been an erosion of social values. As traditional and postwar values recede, so does the mortar that holds this nation together. The soul of Japan is up for grabs.

Spiritual Hunger

Freedom of movement, money for luxuries, free time, and "marriage for love" characterize this generation. Gone are long hours at the office, formal dress and speech, arranged marriages, and scrimping for the future. Today's younger Japanese are also spiritually hungry.

New Age religions sweep the country as people replace the materialism of the postwar years with a craving for life in the inner man. This climate makes it easy to bring young people to a knowledge of the Lord. The problems start when you try to introduce them to church. The churches in Japan are traditional and closed to outsiders. This is why the average attendance in Japanese churches is 29 people. It also explains why there are twice as many Christians as there are church attenders in Japan. A recent survey shows that the number who claim to be Christians is close to three percent while attendance tallies come in at less than one percent. Many non attenders are younger people or those who found Christ while studying abroad. To most of them, Japanese churches are unfriendly, too traditional, and irrelevant to their personal needs.

Fitting In

A friend of mine recently returned to Japan after becoming a Christian in our church. She tried three churches but could find none that seemed loving. I asked one of the pastors she visited about her experience. She had told me that someone in his church strongly criticized her for laughing too loud. His response was to lecture me on how important it is to "examine new people carefully to see if they really fit into our church or not." This attitude is far removed from Jesus' admonition to go to the highways and bring them in. Churches are often judgmental and more reminiscent of the Pharisees than of the early Christians. The Christian church ought to be the most loving and accepting group of people in Japan.

The inability to integrate young people threatens the very existence of Christianity in Japan. There are few new members to replace those who die. Not enough young pastors to assume pulpits left empty by retirement. One group freely admits that three-fourths of their pastors will retire during the next 10 years. They acknowledge that they have no replacements. Worse, there is no plan to find any.

A Thread of Hope

In spite of all the gloom, the future does contain a thread of hope. Social disintegration is breaking the stronghold of tradition. Any young leaders who do emerge will help free the churches from the death of institutionalism. The worldwide church growth movement is beginning to impact Japanese Christian leaders. Some now compare church and denominational traditions to Scripture and ask, "Why are we doing things this way?"

Because the current system is threatened with extinction, it may change. Church culture could adjust itself enough to communicate with the next generation. Several prominent pastors are beginning to ponder biblical principles for growth. These ideas include focused evangelism, loving fellowship and cultural accommodation. They are learning what the apostle Paul meant about becoming all things to all men so he could win some (1 Corinthians 9:22-23).

BRIDGE BUILDERS

Besides Corey, Jeff, and John, another tireless apostle of change in Japan is Steve Fox. Steve is a well-known Japanese rock musician and evangelist. His background in Japan's secular music gives him a unique voice among younger leaders. As a result of his ministry, several young pastors are planting churches tailored specifically to the needs of the young. Churches that have already done this are growing rapidly and other, more senior, pastors are taking notes. The success of one man breeds courage in another.

We've enjoyed great success in several such ventures. Pastor Rob Flaherty and his team at Kobe Bible Fellowship serve nearly 200, mostly young, Japanese Christians. Theirs is the largest evangelical congregation in that city. They are busy planting churches in nearby Rokko Island and to the west in Hiroshima. Sugiyoshi and Eri Suzuki reach about 40 young couples and college students in Life Chapel, near Fujisawa. Andy Nagahara pastors a similar congregation called "Your Church" in Machida City. These churches cluster together and encourage one another. Another forward-thinking pastor in Machida is Yoshinobu Uchimura.

Ross Yamauchi from our own congregation planted Hope Chapel Waseda in the heart of Tokyo. His very street-smart congregation reminds me of Hermosa Beach in the early days. Add Junji Ono pastoring a Japanese congregation called Bridge of Hope in Honolulu; Corey Grinder in Tokorozawa; Jeff MacKay in Osaka and John Bacigalupo in Naha, Okinawa. We've been busy in Japan. Each of these church planters has vision for a string of churches. Folks like them will write the future history of Christianity in Japan.

We should pray for grassroots leadership that can embrace the future. We need leaders who can address a society that claims the Bible as its best-selling book and is building Christian wedding chapels into all of its major hotels. Japan is spiritually hungry, and the interest in Christianity is high. Interest in church, however, as currently presented, is low. If we change our approach, the much-anticipated and often-prophesied revival may eventually occur.

There is hope on the horizon. Several new churches have burst on the scene in the past few years. Their members evangelize easily and naturally. Everyone is welcomed regardless of station in life. The music, while distinctly Japanese, carries heavy rock strains. Most important, the Bible is at the center of attention and formulates a foundation for life and worship.

THE PROBLEM OF WINESKINS

Jesus told us that you cannot put new wine into old wineskins without breaking the skins. He spoke of leather wine bottles that could no longer stretch to accommodate the expansion that accompanies fermenting wine. The comparison is obvious. Older churches have their own tradition and heritage. It would invite disaster to fill them with the fresh work of the Spirit in a new generation.

The older congregations are filled with faithful people and you would never want to destroy them. At the same time, we must evangelize the young. For this reason we hope to see hundreds, perhaps thousands of new churches in Japan during the coming years.

13

TAKING THE LAND

In 1988 our Kaneohe church council felt we should pursue land for a church building. The first plan was to build a chapel for a nearby college. We would use the facility on weekends. They could have it during the week. It seemed like a great idea, but they wanted a gym instead of a chapel.

Plan Two was to build a strong savings account or "building fund." We had no land or visibility of land, yet we would begin saving by faith . . . faith that God would provide land for sale. At the time it seemed really naive. We "knew" there was no land available in Kaneohe. We had searched tax maps and approached several owners to no avail.

FAITH FOR THE FUTURE

During the spring, we sought God and approached our primary leaders with the idea of starting a building fund rooted in faith alone. After much prayer, they decided to go for it. A group of concerned people put together a project called "Faith for the Future." Lasting 100 days from beginning to climax, this project would provide a detailed illustration of the need for land and buildings. We knew that people would give if they understood our needs and the potential for greater evangelism. Our church family is generous and loves to give when the giving produces healthy benefits for the church and community.

Prayer was the key to our success. We never asked people to give. They were simply to pray for guidance as to their participation in the project. We spent the spring of 1988 communicating the need for a church building and asking people to speak to God about it. We wanted them to ask the Lord what he would challenge them to give above their normal tithes and offerings. Our slogan was "A God-inspired sacrifice, a God-supplied gift." We would trust the Lord to challenge us to give beyond our comfort zone. Whatever he said to give would be the *God-inspired sacrifice*. In faith, we would then trust him to supply the amount he specified. Hence, the *God-supplied gift*.

The church responded wonderfully. At a banquet in the Ilikai Hotel, we held a night of praise and worship and collected "commitment cards," pledging financial gifts toward the building fund. Nearly every person in the church showed up. It became a night of reverence and wonder just to experience the heavy atmosphere of love in that room. At the end of the evening, people promised nearly $900,000 toward the building.

LAND HO!

That dinner occurred in May of 1988. Four months later, God supplied land for the project.

I arrived in my office one morning to find a real estate listing on my desk. Someone was offering to sell a 54-year lease for nine acres of land on the side of a mountain overlooking Kaneohe Town and Bay. I was really shocked. We had approached many landowners, asking them to sell. People *never* came to us offering to sell. God was at work. He challenged our faith and then acted in response to it. As soon as we began to save for it, he provided a place for our church home. I am reminded of Jesus' promise that the Father will answer every prayer so the fruit of ministry will remain (John 15:16).

By January 1989 we obtained the right to use that land for the next two generations. Our people accelerated their giving and the land became ours. The cost—just $300,000. It's a lease and we hope to purchase it in the distant future. But for now it is ours, and we got it at a price we could certainly afford. God's timing of the fund-raising campaign and the offer to lease couldn't have been more precise.

A TIME OF STRUGGLE

The immediate result of the land lease was a struggle with the City and County of Honolulu, the State of Hawaii, and our immediate neighbors. Zoning and traffic issues loomed large. The land was zoned as agricultural and would allow for church occupancy. However, it was adjacent to a residential neighborhood so traffic was a concern. To make a long story much shorter, it took more than nine years to gain permission to put the first shovel in the ground.

During those years, I used to pray over the property every time I drove past it on my way into Honolulu. I was often reminded of the dark days in Hermosa Beach when it looked like we had lost the bowling alley. This time, though, my thoughts were different. They were filled with faith. Because of the disappointment and then ultimate victory in Hermosa, my faith was stronger. My life fit the character development plan that the apostle Paul gave to the Christians in Rome (Romans 5:1-5). This wonderful Scripture reminds us that we have become friends of God. As friends, even our difficulties work for our benefit because he is on our side. The tough times are designed to build character, perseverance, and hope. Ultimately, the hope will not disappoint us or leave us embarrassed, because of the love of God. Looking back, I could easily see the difficulty in Hermosa Beach as one of those character-building times. It wasn't too great a stretch to view the current difficulty as another of those builders of perseverance and hope.

No Access

However, my faith did have its limits. While we were ultimately told that we could construct the facility, the city would not allow us to drive through the neighborhood to access the property. This was particularly hard to swallow since we were part owners of the roads in that neighborhood as our land was a portion of the original development. The roads were privately held, not a part of the city. This decision came after the neighbors staged a "drive-in." They staged this event for the TV evening news. They assembled nearly a hundred cars and trucks and drove up and down the access road, honking and creating a great deal of confusion. Cars were parked on both sides of the road to make the situation tighter. The mayor, Frank Fasi, went for the display and denied us access. My faith level ebbed to an all-time low.

To make matters worse, I had spent plenty of time hiking the land. I was now convinced that this was the location where I had been standing with that crowd of people in the original vision which sent us to Hawaii. But, it seemed that God might not be able to help us with a building permit. Of course, those fears were strongest in the depth of the night. During the days, I clung to his promises and held out for the victory we all expected. I did not, however, tell anyone that I now viewed this piece of real estate as the same land I had seen in the vision.

One impetus to faith was a man named Bryant Smith. A semi-retired heavy equipment operator, he felt God had called him to help us turn a steep mountain into a church home. Bryant is a former U.S. Navy sailor who helped reconstruct the cities of Japan in the aftermath of World War II. No project seemed too large for him. He lives in California and spends time building and operating an orphanage in Oklahoma. We got to know him through his daughter and son-in-law who are strong members of our church. Bryant would always show up just when our faith needed a boost. His faith was so strong, and he was so blunt, that we viewed him as a prophetic messenger who happened to have a great sense of humor. Bryant would also save us a couple of million dollars when construction finally began.

Help from Heaven

Before we could build anything, we needed permits. At a city-wide prayer meeting for pastors, I met Victor Borgia, a man I had previously known only by reputation. Victor offered to contact Mayor Fasi on our behalf. It turned out that he held a private Bible study for several members of the mayor's family and staff. His efforts paid off. The mayor went to work on the governor and we were granted a lease on 2.5 acres of land adjacent to ours and not affecting our neighbors. This quarter-mile long and 32-foot-wide strip of land would become our access road. It brought our total campus to just under 12 acres. One of the largest church building sites in Oahu. God's timing is miraculous: Victor moved to heaven within three months of our first conversation. He was felled by a rapidly growing tumor. By the time the doctors discovered it, he had only a couple of weeks to live. In the short time we knew him, he became a major player in the future history of our church.

Help from City Hall

Frank Fasi did us another favor. He introduced us to his city managing director, Jeremy Harris. Mr. Harris became a helpful ally during those early days of the project. His help grew far more important after he became mayor himself. Mayor Harris campaigned for refined and effective government. Speeding up the building process is one of his major contributions to city life. Our project with its many *speed bumps* became an important issue to him. He is a good friend. Without his help, we would not occupy our church campus.

Problems as Blessings

One of our greatest challenges recast itself as a beneficial tool. The state and city governments miscalculated the volume of rainwater that passes over our land. No big deal by itself, this became a huge issue to the homeowners the city allowed immediately below our land. Their street sewers and the drains on our property were not large enough to carry the runoff. Bad enough by itself, the threat multiplied when the government built the H-3 freeway above us. That project acted as a large dam concentrating mountain runoff and funneling it onto our land. We also got drainage from the surface of the elevated freeway lanes. To prevent massive flooding in the neighborhood, we built an underground reservoir the size of a large gymnasium. It lays 25 feet under our largest parking lot. Its cost equaled one-seventh of the entire project.

How did such a burden become a blessing? One day, Rob McWilliams walked the undeveloped site with a group of state engineers. He asked them to financially compensate us for the cost of the reservoir. They admitted liability and the very real danger of a flash flood. Warning us not to pursue legal action, they promised action on our need for a new road. They would speed along the mayor's request that the governor help us with leased land for a road. In other words, surrendering our rights over the drainage headache smoothed the way for the road lease. An ancient author magnified God for performing miracles without number and great works which are too marvelous to understand (Job 19:10). We rejoiced with him when we finally understood that our largest construction problem was a key to unlock the door to our even greater political problem.

Building the road was no picnic. It consumed another one-seventh of our total costs. Obtaining a right of way was one thing, gaining permission to build was another. We faced huge physical and environmental obstacles. Physically, the terrain was so difficult that a hike of the future quarter-mile roadbed took healthy men over an hour and a half. And that was if we avoided the 15 yards of waste-deep swamp. The road would traverse a wetland. It required an environmental impact study which could consume another five years. The Army Corps of Engineers (the governing authority in this matter) allowed us to use their own study prepared for the primary access road into our neighborhood. That decision saved money as well as time.

Wetlands are sacred in modern America. To build on them, we had to replace them. This could mean buying vacant land and constructing ponds and a wildlife sanctuary.

God came to our aid, once again. Windward Community College and the Hawaii State Hospital are our next neighbors, across the wetland. We were able to build a wet-taro farm on hospital land. This production of the root used in the production of *poi* would benefit all three parties. We gained the ability to replace the wetlands we were paving. The college gained an important asset for their Hawaiian Studies Program. The hospital found benefit in a work-therapy program for their patients. There is an added blessing. Public schools will use this living laboratory as a destination for field trips. Students will experience their heritage as they observe *and* participate in the production of this food staple, so important to our heritage.

DIRT, DIRT, AND LOTS MORE DIRT

Construction crews hauled dirt off the site for two-and-a-half years. In all, they carried nearly 5,000 large truckloads of the stuff away. We were fortunate in that the construction of nearby Bay View Golf Course required lots of fill-dirt. They paid the cost of hauling. Their participation subtracted nearly 10 percent of the projected cost of the project. In addition to turning a steep mountain into a series of buildable plateaus, construction crews lowered the overall height of the land by 12 feet. Describing the enormity of effort is impossible. Cal Kim, our civil engineer, and Bryant Smith, the excavation superintendent, provided masterful wisdom. They made the impossible merely difficult.

HOME AT LAST

February 1998 saw the office staff relocated to the site. Crews of volunteers assembled beautiful temporary offices from construction trailers. Beautiful decks and lovely landscape contrasted with earthmoving that dirtied cars and shook walls. But the sense of ownership and homecoming overshadowed the hardships. An added benefit was the rent money saved by moving. Our church headquarters had previously been in a series of spaces in commercial office buildings. We began life overlooking the ocean and a beautiful canal in Kailua's Pali Palms Plaza. Growth forced us to move to three different locations within that structure. The nearby Yum Yum Tree restaurant was our annex for counseling and meetings. Buying food from them was less expensive than renting larger facilities. For five years we were located in a small Kaneohe building located above a good delicatessen. Again the combination of office and restaurant helped conserve funds. Our third location was the Castle Professional Center in the heart of Kaneohe. The landlord was the Seventh Day Adventist Church. The management team was great and easy to work with. They often joint-ventured with us and the Kaneohe Police Department to co-sponsor community service projects. These included efforts to clean graffiti, parental drug awareness campaigns, and efforts to combat illiteracy among children.

Church in a Tent

May 1999 saw the congregation installed on our new church campus. This was possible due to innovation, imagination, and the work of hundreds of volunteers. The original plan called for development of the property in stages. We would build infrastructure and save money. When the funds were strong enough, we would raise a nice building. It all turned out differently.

In 1996 we built the underground reservoir. The construction created a large enough flat space for our annual *Ho'olaulea*, or church picnic. We had a great time. Fearing rain, our staff rented huge tents to protect the crowd of more than 2,000 people in case of rain. The weather was dry, rendering the tents quite useless . . . to all except Chuck Heitzman. He saw them from another angle. His suggestion was that we purchase a tent and move the church onto the property as soon as possible. We could save thousands of dollars each month and enjoy the early use of the land. He felt people would be more motivated to give if they could use the facility while we saved for a permanent structure.

A quick tour of the Internet produced some very nice 'tents.' Technically termed "membrane structures," this class of construction costs one-tenth of what it would take to erect a simple wood-frame building. We chose a company that could meet the height restrictions dictated by our location, adjacent to a residential neighborhood. It's become a lovely home for our congregation. Actual construction of the "clamshell" took only 10 days, effectively doubling our capacity to house people.

It was innovative as well. Though nearly 90 of these structures were already in use in Hawaii, ours became the first to be built under a permit from the building department. All other uses were by government agencies that don't require permits. Because we were first, we set a precedent for all who would follow. Innovation often takes time. Being first meant jumping through extra hoops. But the frustration was offset by the knowledge that we were, perhaps, pioneering a tool which would benefit other churches.

Another innovation found its way into the construction of our many and massive retaining walls. Nearly 20 large retaining walls define the shape of our church campus. We built them with concrete blocks held together by fiberglass pins instead of mortar, concrete and steel. The blocks, each weighing 95 pounds, can be assembled by unskilled volunteers. The volunteers were faithful and productive. The savings were immense. Those blocks, if lain side to side in one long strip, would stretch for more than nine miles. For two years, most Saturdays and weekday evenings saw up to 100 people laying block and planting groundcover for our new location.

SEVEN "FATAL FLAWS"

Our architectural team had warned us: "The site has seven *fatal* flaws. Seven major problems, any of which can kill the entire project. You will never build on this site." The Lord conquered all seven. Today we sit high above Kaneohe town. The view is astounding. You can see all of Kaneohe Bay and much of the Windward coast on one side. Kailua town and the Ko'olau mountains are visible in the opposite direction. The fact of the physical beauty seems to overcome the price we paid in anxiety along the way. But there is another spectacular benefit:

The fulfillment of a prophecy. Not only is this the location which I saw in the vision that moved me to Hawaii, but it brings Jack Hayford's prophecy to physical reality. We have become that coconut tree planted on a hill overlooking the city. And like the tree in that prophecy, we are reproductive. While waiting to move we've reproduced ourselves, over and over again.

Our spiritual sojourn taught us the importance of waiting on God. Isaiah wrote that those who wait for him will rise on wings as eagles (see Isaiah 40:31). We certainly did not go without God's blessing during the waiting process. Just as the nation of Israel matured during their time in the wilderness, we grew stronger as we waited for our own home. Waiting is good. Not fun, just good.

Ross Yamauchi and members of Hope Chapel Waseda in Tokyo. Strong in evangelism and filled with kids off the street, this church is much like Hope Chapel in the earliest days.

Kelly and Angie Hilderbrand planted Hope Chapel Honolulu in the early 1990s they are now Foursquare missionaries in Thailand.

Rob Flaherty is pastor of 200 member Kobe Bible Fellowship, our most successful church plant in Japan. The church is filled with young people every Sunday and actively discipling pastors and planting daughter churches.

Loyd Flaherty and Shun Kurisaka from Hope Chapel Tokorozawa leading worship in an early Kobe Bible Fellowship meeting.

L to R: Jeff MacKay planted Hope Chapels in Mililani, and Osaka. Carl Moore pastors over 100 high schoolers in Huntington Beach. John Honold planted Hope Chapel Kapolei and disciples pastors all over the United States and Japan.

Corey and Lisa Grinder watch as their daughters Kailie and Malia tell us what life is like as Missionaries in Japan. Corey pastors Hope Chapel Tokorozawa and is Tokyo Supervisor for the Japan Foursquare Churches.

A "Bridge Team" from Japan coming to Hawaii for training in leadership and church planting.

A recent photo caught the Hope Chapel Kaneohe staff team taking a breather at a local water-sports park.

Volunteers labor at construction of one of the many massive retaining walls for our new church campus. Lain end to end, the concrete blocks would stretch for just under ten miles.

The "tent" or membrane structure went up in just fourteen days.

The new church campus offers plenty of space for a growing congregation and ministry resource center.

Two weeks prior to occupying our new campus, we launched Hope Chapel Olomana, sending out more than twenty percent of our congregation. But, the new auditorium is rapidly filling to capacity.

Ross Yamasaki and Walter Santiago being sent out to plant Hope Chapel Koʻolauloa in Kahuku, Oahu. They minister to ten percent of the population of their community.

1997 worship band: Michelle and Randall Kalama are first and third from the left. The big guy between them is Guy Kapeliela who would go on to plant Hope Chapel Olomana in Kailua.

This photo shows five generations of church planters in New Hampshire. Ralph commissioned Dale Yancy who sent out Tom Johnston. Tom sent Joe Mabe who launched Robert Haynes. This kind of succession is our best success.

Moore family including Kelly's husband-to-be, Travis White, at grand-daughter Kylie's first birthday luau. Kanani is holding the birthday girl.

14

GROWING TO MATURITY

Not long ago our federal government crudely attempted to restore the importance of families. An entire year was dubbed the "Year of the Family." It was a hollow gesture to cover the pain of broken homes. The United States has more broken families, per capita, than any other developed country. A few months into the fanfare, the news media began reporting the growing absence of fathers in American families. Awareness is power, but knowledge of this situation didn't seem to help much.

For decades, lots of lower income and inner-city families lived without fathers present in their homes. Our welfare system punished couples for maintaining a normal household. Single mothers were, justly, a target of support. But, the structure backfired. A man found living in a home caused payments to be reduced or shut off. By 1960, 17 percent of American children had no father at home. Few alarms rose until middle- and upper-income families began to experience the results of fatherless homes. At first, the phenomenon was explained as a product of divorce and male abandonment of responsibility. The upswing in babies out of wedlock was buried in abortion statistics for a few years. Abortion numbers are falling and more children are raised without dads. Today's twist is a little different. Many women want children, but lack trust toward men because of pain in their own past. Men are increasingly seen as sperm-donors, unnecessary to the parenting process. The change from one millennium into another marked 40 percent of American homes as fatherless.

REAPING THE PAST

We currently reap the harvest of our past excesses. We declared God dead in the '60s. We embraced "sex, drugs and rock 'n' roll" in the '70s. Money was king during the '80s. Internet IPOs and a raging stock market dominated the '90s. For decades, kids and family never meant much in America. The divorce rate skyrocketed without hindrance.

Divorce destroyed 20 percent of marriages in the early 1960s. By 1990 the rate of destruction escalated to nearly 50 percent. Broken families inflict more damage on children than on adults. Girls living in fatherless homes are nearly three times as likely as those living with their dads to become pregnant as teenagers. Boys without fathers are more than twice as likely to get into crime or drop out of school. Youth gangs and racial hatred seem out of control in the new millennium. This is the result of families dying when Americans threw over God and his standards for our culture.

Unless God does something wonderful, the American family will be an institution of the past. Yet we hope for miracles. A good church can go a long way toward reducing the damage of divorce. Revivals turn cultures around. Churches turn individual lives around through God's word and power. God is at work in our church and thousands of others. He said he would place the homeless into families. We believe that begins with a healthy *spiritual* family.

NETWORKING A SPIRITUAL FAMILY

All the counseling in the world adds up to nothing without sustaining love from people nearby. Most troubled people in our society come from damaged families. We are here to help them. Our church exists to train ordinary people to do God's work. More simply put, we are here to teach our people to *help others* gain control over their lives through God's redeeming and accepting love. We are raising an army to love the broken. The task is usually costly and often difficult, but always simple—with one hand reach out to Jesus, with the other bring a friend. The message—of a God who forgives, made personal through people who know how to love, will heal the heart of our nation.

Love involves people. Therefore, people are always the focus of a healthy church. Buildings or programs can never drive the congregation if it is to fulfill its purpose. However, ministries to hurting people must have purpose and structure. Churches serve people at every stage of life. Younger people tend to cluster around people their own age. After folks reach their mid-20s, however, they seem to want to be with people of other generations. This makes for a strong church. We approach this through our network of life-stage MiniChurches. Lisa Kai and Sandra Murakami begin the list, looking after hundreds of children and a hundred leaders in our Children's Church which looks much like a traditional Sunday School. Tom Landeza oversees nearly a hundred junior high students. Mike Kai and his team oversee a large public meeting called "The Well" and operate a thriving group of high school MiniChurches. Tisha Falcon and Jeph Chavez run an ever-growing network of singles MiniChurches. Al Kalama, Connie Haskell and Rob McWilliams keep the rest of us busy in groups designed to meet needs of men, women, and families. Meanwhile, people like Allan Lau build ministry teams to support our weekend services. Drama groups, worship bands, ushers, greeters, and parking lot attendants tend to find strength of fellowship with their partners in the task they accomplish every week. Our goal is for every member of our church to have a small group of Christians he or she can count on for friendship, personal accountability, as well as support in times when life gets rough. While the American family breaks down, the church can, and should, fill the void through meaningful small group relationships.

MINICHURCH & MATURITY

Pastors are forever asking me, "How do you build personal accountability into Christians who live in a country that shuns the concept?" My answer always involves MiniChurch. I first discovered the blessing of small groups early in the life of the Hermosa Beach congregation. You will remember that I wrote of the early Bible studies which formed building blocks to that tiny congregation on Manhattan Beach Boulevard. Later, a small group structure allowed us to maintain overall unity while we tried to integrate four groups of Christians who each identified with their own leader. Finally, the MiniChurch concept took on its productive shape in the year after we moved into the bowling alley. It wasn't until moving to Hawaii that we linked this powerful and loving small group experience to personal spiritual accountability. Because we've learned so much in recent years, I want to revisit the concept of MiniChurch in the next few paragraphs. My desire is to take you, as a reader, beyond the simple small group concept into the idea of Christians ministering to "one another." Most American churches are built around the gifts of one strong leader. By contrast, a quick look through a Bible concordance reveals how often the New Testament stresses the need for members of Jesus' family to minister to one another. The biblical model is that of shared ministry involving each member as care giver on one occasion and care receiver on the other.

I've always been leery of "accountability churches." These are the churches where leaders talk about personal accountability all the time. But, they really function as a *dictatorship* where a select few make decisions about everyone else's lives. I never want to participate in a church like that. The polar opposite of accountability churches are those which preach personal freedom to the extreme that all honest *personal* accountability vanishes, people can interpret God's grace as a cover for an "anything goes" lifestyle. The message of grace and unconditional love needs the counterweight of accountability to personal holiness. For us, MiniChurch grew to provide a balance between the two. It is in this balance that lives are being changed. Broken lives from broken families are finding peace. Our people are growing to maturity in Christ as they apply the Scriptures to their daily lives.

Scheduled Sharing

Our concept of accountability centers on the Bible. The weekend Bible teaching becomes a curriculum for the Mini-Churches that meet all over Oahu each week. We get together for a relaxed evening of food, fellowship, Bible and life discussion, and prayer. It feels much like a family reunion except that it centers on the Scriptures.

While some of our MiniChurches begin with worship choruses, I like to spend the first 20 minutes or so letting people enjoy each other's fellowship while eating snack foods. The goal is to decompress from the day's activities and people seem to talk better over food. This also allows latecomers to arrive without disturbing more serious discussion. The food up front sometimes saves the evening for a person who was required to work so late that they had no time for dinner. Food is followed by about five minutes where we throw out single sentence reminders of the previous weekend sermon. This helps everyone bring the message out of the file cabinet of memory and back on the table of discussion. Discussion of the sermon gets the next 45 minutes of our time. In reality, we don't discuss the sermon. Rather we hold our lives up to the Scripture we studied under the pastor's guidance. Our feeling is that most Christians are hearers of God's word. Our goal is to become doers as well (James 1:22). We think of church much like a spiritual university. The weekend teaching is the lecture. MiniChurch becomes the *laboratory*. The MiniChurch leaders are taught that they should never dominate the discussion. Their job is to coach the rest of the team into ministering to one another. As a result, burdens are shared by a number of people; spiritual gifts surface and mature; pastors become equippers of God's people who learn to do his work. One side benefit to this approach is that no one feels an urgency to "get through the outline." If pressing needs arise, the whole group will focus its energies on supporting a single individual. The end of the evening is marked with prayer. No requests, just prayer for issues that surface during the fellowship and life application Bible study. People are asked to pray aloud around the circle. They pray for one or two things that touched their heart concerning others in the room. Their prayer becomes a promise to remember to pray for that person throughout the following seven days. In this scenario, the MiniChurch leader functions as a coach. The members are the players.

A Family of Families

This simple format has transformed our congregation into a family of families. Nearly 60 percent of our people are involved in MiniChurch. The pastoral counseling load is vastly reduced as people share each other's burdens (Galatians 6:2). More importantly, people are rediscovering a sense of family and accountability to God and themselves. Lives are simply and powerfully transformed. We've seen marriages restored. Some are set free from addictions. The power of sexual perversion is broken through the confession of sin and follow up prayer. Parenting skills get passed on from healthy families to young people raised without healthy role models. Couples have met and married through the MiniChurch experience. The MiniChurch family provides support when its members move, are hospitalized, etc. We think we found the key to all this success the day we switched to studying our own lives in the light of the Scriptures discussed in the previous sermon. At that point, God's word actually became a searchlight illuminating and freeing our hearts.

MINISTRY GROWS FROM MINICHURCH

MiniChurch produces leaders. We identify the leader of each small *flock* as a shepherd or *pastor*. These budding pastors and their apprentices train in a study group twice a month. They meet to discuss a teaching based on whatever book they might be studying at the time. Some of our current leaders have gone through more than 60 books while training with our pastoral staff. The first half of the meeting centers on the text. The second half of the evening provides an opportunity for everyone present to air out whatever ministry problems they currently face. The MiniChurch pastors training meetings provide both theological and practical training for current and future leadership. Our cadre of MiniChurch pastors and their apprentices is the talent pool we search when hiring paid staff. Every staff member and every church planter we've launched first proved their ability as a successful MiniChurch pastor.

Gateways to Freedom

Some people bring specialized problems to church. They often need help in the form of a specialized MiniChurch. A few years ago our staff and MiniChurch pastors had the fun of hearing Ted Roberts, the current pastor of the Easthill Church in Gresham, Oregon. He told of a ministry in their church aimed at freeing people from pornography and other sexual addictions. From it had grown a larger set of ministries focusing on various life-dominating sins. Ted's teachings struck a chord in the heart of one woman—a MiniChurch leader named Patience Boersma. She had early life problems with alcohol. God had set her free and in Ted's presentation she saw the possibility of freedom for others.

Obtaining curriculum materials from Easthill, Patience combined our MiniChurch concept with their ministry model. From the mix, *Gateways to Freedom* was born. Gateways are MiniChurches which begin their life targeting people suffering from a specific set of temptations *or* reaching out to people who have suffered as a result of other people's sins. A typical Gateways MiniChurch will begin with curriculum materials, later moving on to function more like our other MiniChurches. The goal is to deal with the larger sin problems and then integrate into normal patterns of Christian life and family. Again, we are providing *intentional* families in a society where family is weak or lacking.

An early victory of Gateways ministry is on display in the lives of Blair and Nalani Hanna. Drawn to church through marital difficulty, they always sat on the front row. He looked menacing. She appeared hurt. One evening I spoke on the problem of abuse and violence in marriage. At the close of the service Nalani approached me to ask how to deal with an abusive husband. It was all too obvious that she was not asking a hypothetical question. Blair soon interrupted our discussion. His question, "Is she telling you about me?" When I told him she was, he proceeded to say, "Then you better pay close attention, because everything she says is true!" He then abruptly walked off, leaving me with his sobbing wife. That night was a breakthrough for both of them. The veil of secrecy was torn. They had the opportunity to find real freedom. She began meeting with Patience and others. He soon accepted Jesus as his *Lord*. Today, both are strong leaders helping others to the freedom they found. The night Blair opened up, a young man named Reyn Uehara sent the teaching tape to his sister in California. She had suffered physical abuse for several years. Upon listening to the tape, she flew to Hawaii and accepted the Lord in our church. She too spent time in the Gateways ministry and in MiniChurch. Today, she is married to a great guy named Keith Yoshimoto and serves as the women's pastor in our high school ministry. To me, these people signify the natural progression every person ought to make in every church. We all come to the church as if it were a hospital for the spiritually sick. In time, we should grow beyond *patient* status and become members of the healing team.

Straight Street Resource Center

Another blessing resulting from MiniChurch is our *Straight Street Resource Center.* It is run by Wendell Elento, a former naval officer and graduate of the United States Naval Academy; Debra Grant, my former secretary; and Ron Chambers, our media producer. Straight Street is the publication arm of our church, and of the Hope Chapel- birthed churches throughout the world. We rapidly multiply leaders in a church with unique ministries. Many of them go on to plant churches. Both our unique ministry style and the speed of reproduction have necessitated the development of new tools. No one else designs curriculum and materials fitted to our purpose. Out of this need Straight Street was born.

Saul of Tarsus found sight and spiritual insight at the hands of a simple Christian named Ananias. The scales were lifted from his eyes in a home on a lane called Straight Street (Acts 9:11). Our goal is to help people find vision for world-reaching ministry. Straight Street Resources is dedicated to that process.

Straight Street came into life in response to a demand for materials to strengthen Christian leaders. We first developed a couple of audiocassette albums teaching how to plant churches and how to build a network of small groups. Soon we realized that we needed to organize to better service the people calling for help. Tools range from the book you are reading to audio and video tape seminars helping pastors develop leaders and plant churches. In between, there are weekly sermon tapes, music CDs, and curriculum helps for courses taught in local congregations. Everything was designed with our own members in mind first. Our commitment is to feed our flock and trust Jesus to build his church, in others, through our effort. The result is a practicality that you can *feel* when you use the material. The addition of our website has expanded our ability to distribute materials. Free access to the web cuts publishing costs and even allows us to give away white papers and weekend teachings at no charge.

Christian Life Development and The Pastor Factory
Two other resources evolving in our church include a quarterly teaching series called *Christian Life Development (CLD)* and a

bimonthly training event for MiniChurch leaders which we call the *Pastor Factory*.

CLD exists to help busy Christians learn to lead within the context of their homes, in the workplace and in the church. This is the place for people who want to know more about God and his plans and purposes for their lives. After that it becomes a tooling location for expanded ministry. Sessions generally last for four hours on a Saturday morning or Sunday afternoon. These events replace weekly teaching series. We found our people too involved with life to attend four or six consecutive weeks of anything. Many of our people work both a full-time *and* a part-time job in Hawaii's anemic economy. We adapted to their needs by moving our training schedule toward their free time.

The *Pastor Factory* is the granddaddy of teaching venues in our Kaneohe church. This bimonthly event runs *off-cycle* to the Tuesday evening MiniChurch Shepherds training venue. The entire full-and part-time pastoral staff meets in my home for a couple hours of discipleship.

We go over the same books that are being studied by the MiniChurch shepherds. The difference is that, in this meeting, I am privileged to instruct the people who teach and coach our MiniChurch Shepherds. This keeps me fresh. It also keeps me responsible for making disciples. We spend one half of the evening studying the material to be taught the following week. The rest of the time goes toward directly discipling these leaders of leaders in pastoral ministry. Finally, it is here that the most experienced of our leadership gather for refinement and vision. These are the people who leave us to launch all those new churches.

BIG, BAD GUY

An exciting example to the effectiveness of this "training without end" is found in the life of Guy Kapeliela. He recently planted Hope Chapel Olomana in Kailua about six miles from us.

Guy is an extremely large and formerly violent man. In his drug infested days, he was the fear of both Kaneohe and Kailua. Uncertain of himself, violence and intimidation were the only tools he understood when engaging other people. His troubled adolescence eventually got topped off with a forfeited football scholarship at a mainland university. This was enough to send Guy on a spiritual search. He ended up in our church, invited by Aaron Suzuki and Shannon Hill. Aaron lives across the street from Guy's father. He used to hear Guy hollering curses at his dad at all hours of the day and night. Salvation replaced Guy's tough exterior with a shy and soft personality. He became fun to be around, but no leader. Eventually, Guy learned to play the guitar and began helping with worship in his MiniChurch. From there, he graduated to playing in our Friday evening worship band. Illness removed the leader one evening. Guy stepped up to fill his slot and amazed us all. His presence and command of the situation can only be described as gifts of the Holy Spirit. No school could teach a person to radiate love, holiness and leadership as he did that night. Guy could lead—worship.

However, any other sign of leadership skill was lacking. While he was large and imposing to others, to himself he was but a doorkeeper in the house of the Lord. Sunday mornings he arrived two hours early to cart in and set up all the equipment that was necessary to run our Children's Church. Nighttime found him reloading the trucks and shipping containers. It was during this time that someone mentioned to me that Guy felt called to pastor. I was doubtful, but went out of my way to get to know him better.

I discovered a very capable individual. He was holding back because he was embarrassed at his speech and lack of college education. Guy grew up speaking *pidgin,* a blend of Hawaiian and English with a few Japanese words thrown in as well. The grammar may not be textbook English, but it is beautiful to hear and very understandable to any person in the United States. You could compare it to a strong accent found anywhere else—New York, Boston, or the deep South. Nevertheless, his insecurity over language was a huge stumbling block to Guy. Feeling that time spent around our pastoral team would loosen him up, I hired him as my secretary. I had just lost a great secretary to an inter-island move. Any replacement would have seemed deficient. I figured it would be rough going with whomever I hired. So I recruited Guy and quickly discovered that we would have to teach him skills as simple as typing.

He never made much of a secretary. But, the comradery of our staff soon rang his bell. They definitely were not put off by his pidgin. Instead, they began harassing him whenever he tried to correct his grammar or accent. The logic went like this: "You are Hawaiian. Your audience lives in Hawaii. They understand you perfectly. Why change the way you talk . . . you wanna sound stupid?" Constant kidding loosened him up in every area, not just public speaking.

Guy soon became our head worship leader, looking after six worship bands playing each weekend, comprised of more than

100 people. He became Singles Pastor and went on to pastor our Men's Ministry. He shone as a preacher. This, too, involved supernatural gifts of the Holy Spirit. He was great the first time out of the gate. The message was flawless, and its delivery, exciting. Guy is a supreme example of God turning ordinary people into fruitful and productive followers of Jesus Christ. His only formal training for the ministry was our Pastor Factory. Before that, he was as an apprentice leader in MiniChurch and on the worship team. Guy's major contribution to the process was surrender and a hunger to learn. He very ably let go of the ring of pride and anger which he knew as a young man. I am writing this six months into Guy's experience as a church planter. Under his leadership, the new congregation has grown to well over 500 people.

REPRODUCING THE CHURCH

It is always hard to predict success in a pastoral ministry. The best and the brightest incoming students often fall by the wayside. One of the difficulties facing seminaries and other theological training institutes is the dropout rate among graduates. Approximately half of those who enter will graduate. Only about half of those who do graduate from such an institution will actually enter pastoral ministry. Of those who do, nearly 80 percent leave the ministry within the first two years. The remaining 20 percent roughly equals three percent of those who entered the school in the first place. Put differently, this process is 95 percent *ineffective*.

Some have faulted the individual schools. But how could such criticisms be valid if the same set of statistics describes nearly every such school? Most seminaries and Bible schools are filled with dedicated instructors and administrators doing a fine job. Scrutiny soon moves to denominational officials. Maybe they do poorly at integrating young pastors into their structures? Again, if everyone experiences very similar results, there must be a larger, more comprehensive, answer. We think the problem is the same as that of putting carts in front of horses. To us, a theological education is best applied *while* a person is actively engaged in ministry. Our threefold plan works like this: (A) Get a person involved in low levels of Christian service. (B) Promote them into more significant ministry on the basis of faithful and productive service. (C) Add theological education to the mix once a person demonstrates that they are gifted for ministry. Remember, the only defining characteristic of a leader is a *follower.* If a person doesn't have followers, he is no leader. My supposition is that education cannot create a leader. It can only augment and improve one.

Education may come through a continuing process like the Pastor Factory. Or it may be added though tenure as a student in a seminary, for those with enough time and money to obtain this wonderful asset. Either way, educational tools should enhance ministry rather than act as gateways (or bottlenecks) to it. Our combination of ministry assignments plus ongoing mentoring have produced more than 150 pastors. Only about eight percent of those have left the ministry. These results are roughly 10 times more effective than those reported by the system which places schooling before the ministry experience.

Our most productive tool toward reproducing the church has been the MiniChurch. It works like this. A person is seen as an active member, regularly contributing to the well-being of others in the group. He, or she, is then recruited as an apprentice leader. Faithful apprenticeship results in that person moving to pastor a MiniChurch. During apprenticeship and the pastoral years, they are invited to participate in the ongoing MiniChurch training meetings and seminars. Later as they mature, a person will be invited into the Pastor Factory to further sharpen his or her skills. The first result is a highly committed and well-trained cadre of pastoral leadership within our congregation. A second benefit is a group of people with vision to plant a church. These people possess well-developed gifts, skills and knowledge by the time they leave the mother church.

When we launch them as a church planter, we then help them seek further theological training. This way all training is pointed toward enhancing day-to-day ministries. Education at the point of need is always practical and immediately useful. Knowledge, gleaned before entering the fray, remains theoretical. This method keeps our guys practical in both teaching and administration.

CHURCHES AND MORE CHURCHES

Our training programs bear fruit that lasts. Hope Chapel Kaneohe has planted nearly 60 daughter and granddaughter churches in its first 16 years of existence. I haven't time to write in detail about them, but Kean Salzer planted churches in both Oahu and Maui. Chuck Klingman pastors *Our Father's House* which he planted a decade ago. Jim Phillips started Hope Chapel Hawaii Kai, currently pastored by Gordon Horne. Steve Laudise is in Kailua. Leroy Metzger planted Hope Chapel South Shore in Poipu, Kauai. Walter Santiago and Ross Yamasaki birthed Hope Chapel Ko'olauloa in Kahuku, where Walt is a coach of the high school football team. Curtis Blanchette went off to Vancouver, B.C. about the time that Noel and Carol Wilcox started Hope Chapel Coastline in Perth, Australia. Blaine Sato and Carl Moore started Hope Chapel Inland Valley in Chino, California. Kelly and Angie Hilderbrand left Hope Chapel Honolulu in the hands of Terrance Chow and moved to Bangkok where they became pioneer missionaries for the Foursquare Church. Most recently, Rob and Robin Moore (no relation to me) planted Hope Chapel Kalanianaole in east Oahu.

The granddaughter churches are too numerous to name each one. Besides, it seems that every time I turn around, I discover another new church born to the leaders we sent out from our congregation. The growth is rapidly becoming exponential.

20/20 VISION

After beginning with just 12 people in 1972, the Hope Chapel-sponsored churches are estimated to number more than 25,000 people in nearly 150 daughter and granddaughter congregations at the turn of the 21st century. Our *20/20 Vision* is to grow the Hope Chapel family to 500 churches by the year 2020.

Vision is the key word here. No one can *make* this happen. We certainly won't train all the pastors from Kaneohe. We directly plant only one or two churches per year from our congregation. Any higher rate would hinder our own growth and health. We are entirely dependent upon passing the vision on to people in the churches we start and those they start.

Several of our daughter churches have planted multiple numbers of other churches. One series of church plants is worth mentioning here. While I still pastored in Hermosa Beach, Dale Yancy worked as our youth pastor. We eventually sponsored him as a church planter in California's San Fernando Valley. The church was named, *Hope of the Valley*. Later, he left the church with his co-pastor Jeff Fischer. Dale moved to New Hampshire and planted another Hope Chapel. He launched a pastor named Tom Johnston who started a church called Harvest Christian Fellowship in Jaffrey. I am privileged to own a photograph posing myself with Dale, Tom, and two successive church planters who grew out of Tom's ministry. One of those pastors is in process of launching a new church. When he does, we will be able to count six generations of ministry in that single stream. Overall, Tom has established seven new churches since Dale sent him out. Couple that with the fact that Dale, recently launched by Paul Berube and Grace Fellowship in Nashua, is in the midst of a third church he has personally planted. . . . You catch what I am saying about vision. It is catching, ever-expanding, and absolutely necessary if we are going to fulfill the commission to go and make disciples of all the nations (Matthew 28:18-20).

15

LIKE A COCONUT TREE

Do you remember the prophecy I mentioned in earlier chapters? The Lord pictured our church as a coconut tree sitting high on a hill, reproducing itself as it gave off fruit. That tree has become very significant to our church family. We use it as part of our logo. We view it as a metaphor for growing stages within the church. I want to share it with you in the next few paragraphs.

Before we get into the tree as a metaphor for Christian life development, I want to share a humorous story. The move to our new church campus underscored our use of this important teaching tool. When we finally cleared and leveled our land, we discovered a large coconut tree which had grown for years amidst the dense forest. Someone suggested that we should leave it standing in hopes of transplanting it into the landscape design of the finished facility. We never transplanted it. Our architects had no knowledge or consideration of that tree. Unknowingly, they situated our structures and courtyard around its location *and* elevation. When the buildings went up, the tree stood guard just outside our front door. It is the focal point to our entire landscape. It seems that God had something to do with the location of that particular tree 30 years before our construction project.

CHURCH AS A FRUITFUL TREE

To us, the tree speaks of five stages of Christian life development. We challenge our people to "Come grow with us." The idea is to grow to *maturity*. Most Christians talk about "growing in the Lord." Few think in terms of a destination associated with that growth. In all life forms, reproduction is the destination that speaks of maturity. Plants and animals reach maturity when they reach the reproductive stage. Of course, there is much maturing that goes on after reproductive abilities are in full working order, but that is another subject. For our discussion, an organism that never reached the stage of reproductivity is not yet mature. This is a truth in the spiritual world as well as the physical. If our church exists to equip God's people to do his work, we must ask, "What is his work?" His work involves evangelism and church-planting.

Reproduction is part of the basic bargain. Jesus said, "Follow me and I will make you fishers of men" (Matthew 4:19 KJV). Individual Christians are called to reproduce themselves. Later he called the apostles to "go and make disciples of all the nations" (Matthew 28:18-20). The apostles got off to a great start, and today's church leaders are called to complete the task. If you read the Book of Acts as a picture of *normal* church life, you can't escape the successful church in Antioch. It intentionally reproduced itself all over the Mediterranean world. The coconut tree often gives its fruit to the ocean as a means of transportation. A single tree can reproduce itself wherever the tides and currents flow. A church should operate in a similar fashion. It doesn't have to be a coconut tree, all churches are called to reproduce. We should individually and corporately plant seeds of the gospel in whatever soil God provides. This means we must mature until we have the ability to do so. We think that growth comes in five stages:

1. Rooted in God . . . and his Family

The first priority is surrender to the love and forgiveness of Jesus Christ. Salvation and water baptism are starting points for the most basic growth in the Lord. Yet, without roots into a healthy church, most will eventually shrink back. The churches foster growth in a living and personal walk with God through the Scriptures and fellowship with other Christians. Joining a local church requires commitment which naturally feeds and nurtures healthy growth.

2. Growing a Trunk of Authenticity

Every tree needs a strong trunk to stand against the storms of life. Young Christians soon discover the awesome power of God's word—the Bible. Knowledge of the Bible becomes the trunk which supports a successful life and family. This requires that we find a church that actually teaches the word of the Lord. The Scriptures teach that faith grows by our hearing the word of God (Romans 10:17 KJV). In our setting, we not only teach the Scriptures on the weekend, we examine our own lives for authentic Christianity in the discussions we share in MiniChurch. This faithful participation in *both* weekend worship celebrations and MiniChurch are necessary to build a healthy foundation or "trunk" to our spiritual tree.

3. Branching Out in Ministry Skills

It is a mistake to stop growing when you achieve solid Bible knowledge and growing faith. God has some form of ministry on the agenda for every Christian. Healthy Christians participate in ministry. As the leaves of a tree gather light from the sun, we should gather light from the *Son* in the form of specialized knowledge. We should discover our personal spiritual gifts. We should also access any information that would help us use them more skillfully. These gifts are Holy Spirit born abilities which God has invested in each of us (Romans 12:1-11). It is our job to learn how to use them most effectively. Specialized classes and seminars provide the opportunity. Classes teach people how to share their faith. They enhance teaching skills. Some develop counseling or coaching abilities for helping others. In our church, people can learn cross-cultural ministry and how to plant a church. It is up to the individual Christian to grow branches which will take in light, speeding fruitful service. In our setting, CLD Seminars and Fanning the Flame Leadership Conferences help satisfy these needs.

4. Bearing Fruit for the Lord

Jesus said we should testify of him in our hometown, the nearby region and to the ends of the earth (Acts 1:8). The process usually starts with those closest to us: our family and friends. To make a disciple suggests that you help a person become a learner.

5 Stages of
Spiritual Growth

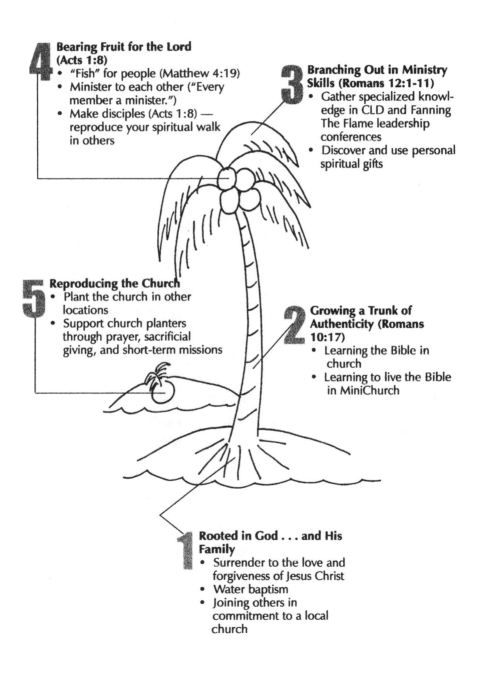

4 **Bearing Fruit for the Lord (Acts 1:8)**
- "Fish" for people (Matthew 4:19)
- Minister to each other ("Every member a minister.")
- Make disciples (Acts 1:8) — reproduce your spiritual walk in others

3 **Branching Out in Ministry Skills (Romans 12:1-11)**
- Gather specialized knowledge in CLD and Fanning The Flame leadership conferences
- Discover and use personal spiritual gifts

5 **Reproducing the Church**
- Plant the church in other locations
- Support church planters through prayer, sacrificial giving, and short-term missions

2 **Growing a Trunk of Authenticity (Romans 10:17)**
- Learning the Bible in church
- Learning to live the Bible in MiniChurch

1 **Rooted in God . . . and His Family**
- Surrender to the love and forgiveness of Jesus Christ
- Water baptism
- Joining others in commitment to a local church

This important task is fairly simple when you possess the right tools. This is why branching out in knowledge is so important.

However, knowledge gained must be put into play to be useful. It is at this fruit bearing stage that the church generates its greatest growth. Normal Christianity should include a mentoring or discipling process for every person. We should all have someone we are learning from. And, we should all have a few people we are helping grow in the Lord.

In my own life away from church, I try to stay in touch with a few non-Christians whom I can challenge with my testimony of Jesus. I also try to maintain relationships with a few Christian young people who I can teach about successful living. Finally, I spend most of my time mentoring my staff and other pastors. Christian life skills are designed to be passed on person to person.

An older pastor once taught me a meaningful slogan: "Every member a minister." I think every member should be equipped to equip others. You will not achieve real health in the Lord until you join with others in sharing the good news of God's love. This can occur in a structured setting like a Bible study. It may happen over cups of coffee among close friends. It should occur in organized ministry within the congregation. However you achieve it, bearing fruit through active ministry is the earmark of a healthy Christian.

5. Reproducing the Church

Hope Chapel is more than a church. It's a movement made up of churches in North America, Asia and the Pacific Islands. Our church is like a coconut tree reproducing itself through many young, sprouting coconuts. Our model is biblical. The New Testament saints went out from Jerusalem on a threefold mission: (A) They preached the gospel wherever they went. (B) They made disciples of their converts. (C) They completed the process by planting new churches. We are carrying on their vision.

Many years ago, I thought we were unique in the calling to plant churches. Today, I believe it is the task of every congregation. We can't be satisfied reproducing ourselves only in individual people. We *must* reproduce the church. Some will say that is a task best left to larger churches. My reply: "We birthed our first daughter church with just 125 people in our congregation." Besides, smaller churches can join with others through denominational or network ties to accomplish the same task. Our denomination, the Foursquare Church, has a wonderful overseas missions program.

By giving to missions outreaches and supporting our friends who leave us to plant churches, we can do ministry in places we will never even visit. We indirectly help evangelize people we will never meet. As followers of Jesus Christ, it is most important that we grow toward maturity. Maturity is marked by reproduction. Without reproduction, we would never be able to effectively evangelize our world and certainly would not meet the spiritual needs of the emerging generations.

The idea of cross-generational ministry is new to some people. They assume that younger people will simply join their elders in worship traditions that have stood the test of time. I believe that a "generation gap" exists today that is as real as that which drove young baby boomers to "never trust anyone over

30" during the late 1960s. We need churches which are flexible enough to present the gospel within the cultural context of rising generations. To me this idea of new churches for a new generation is so important that I wrote an entire book about it called *Friends: How to Evangelize Generation X.*

Reproduction is a sign of maturity in any animal, plant or social system. As we reproduce our church (and our MiniChurches) in other places, we can be sure we are living out the will and mission of God for our lives.

FINDING MY PLACE IN GOD'S FAMILY

A pastor of one of our daughter churches loaned me an idea for a sermon. He asked his people what they thought of a church where: (A) The people didn't love God. They came for other reasons like making business contacts or finding dating partners. (B) The people didn't like or trust their pastors. (C) The people didn't even like each other and would not spend time with their fellow members. (D) As might be expected, they didn't support their church financially through tithes and offerings. (E) Finally, they were too self-centered to actively serve in any ministry capacity.

By now, you realize this pastor's intentions. He set his people up for a challenge to active membership. He was about to challenge his people to grow on to maturity. His very negative story was a springboard to a positive message about church membership. In it he taught the five commitments that we ask of people before inviting them to sign on as members of our congregation. At a heart-level, these commitments open a person to the supernatural touch of the Holy Spirit. It is that touch that transforms ordinary, sin-plagued people into active agents of God's love.

Cost of Membership

Here are the five questions we ask every potential new member:

1. Do you love Jesus Christ and acknowledge him as the Lord of your life and all creation?

Many people come to a church for the fellowship or to meet someone of the opposite sex. I even met a man once who wanted to join our congregation for contacts to support his sales business. Is Jesus the Lord over your life as he is over the church?

2. Do you respect your church leaders and their vision?

In other words, do you feel a sense of *assignment* to this church and its leadership? Assignment suggests a calling: Did God place you in this congregation? If he did not, you should look elsewhere until you discover where you belong. If he did assign you to your church, you should actively seek a role of fruitfulness among your new church family. Churches, like families, have a culture of their own. A congregation's culture is an expression of the personality of the members as they seek the Lord. It also reflects the personality and vision of the leadership. This culture is flavored by the special callings God puts upon each congregation.

Hope Chapel has a unique church culture. It shows in our dress and style of music. It's obvious in our emphasis on the needs of single adults and young families. You can't escape our calling to raise up pastors and plant churches. We spend lots of time addressing a revolution in thought when it comes to the ministry in Japan. These things define us and make us different from other churches.

All of this is too much for some people. There are those who love the Sunday services but don't like our constant talk of Japan. Others prefer fancy buildings to a sacrificial mission to plant churches and care for people who hurt.

I remember a very nice woman who constantly complained about the "rock strains" in our music. Every Sunday she would tell me, "I just love your teaching and the warmth of this church." She would go on to say, "But I may have to leave here because I can't stand that music." I'd just smile and listen to her complain week after week. Finally, I asked what she would do to the music if she could change it. In her answer, she described the music of at least 50 other churches on our island. I told her that I felt she ought to visit around. There are some very good preachers out there and most churches have music she likes.

Most church music is that of a generation ago and younger people don't have it in their hearts. We want to praise God with a true expression of our hearts. You don't ask Japanese-speaking people to sing in English because doing so would hamper their worship. Likewise, we don't ask people of the new millennium to sing the music of the 1980s. It would inhibit their worship.

We have a lot of "young people" with grey hair in our church. Some are in their 70s and early 80s. They feel comfortable with our worship because they would rather serve this generation than sing songs of their own past. I have extra respect for these folks and the love they bring to our church. They are with us because they know God's call in their life. They are willing to do things differently in order to accomplish the command our Lord gave us to preach the gospel to every person.

3. *Are you willing to spend time with the church family?*

Are these your people or do you limit your Christianity to a spectator function? Do you operate from a sense of *ownership*? Ownership indicates that the people and heritage of your church belong to you as well. Your church is a platform that God gave you for living life in community with other Christians. It also becomes a foundation for Christian service. Your church, with all its strengths and weaknesses, belongs to you. You should care for it in prayer and in fellowship. Whether you understand the concept or not, you really own your church.

I believe you should develop at least one serious and solid friendship with another member of your church family. Most people came to church with a friend in the first place. Eighty-seven percent of our people came to our church through the love of a friend. If you join our congregation, we ask you to maintain that friendship and build others. You should involve yourself on a regular basis with those friends and make the Lord a part of your friendship.

This might happen in a MiniChurch or some other study group. It might mean involvement in an organized effort to feed the hungry or regularly visit someone in a convalescent home. You might just meet a friend for lunch on a regular basis. Or perhaps you'll disciple someone while you catch waves like I do occasionally. My limited surfing experience has turned into a wonderful time of friends encouraging each other in the Lord.

You can't be fruitful if you try to live a Christian life outside the context of Christian relationships. Even the Lone Ranger had Tonto. You simply can't "go it alone."

The Bible tells us to "consider how we may spur one another on toward love and good deeds." How are we supposed to do that? "Let us not give up meeting together . . ." (Hebrews 10:24-25). Sunday meetings are great for learning and for worship, but they fall short of allowing you to encourage one another in an exchange of love and friendship. You have to mark out time for others.

4. Do you believe in your church enough to stand with it financially?

I believe in tithing my income. My parents taught me to tithe (give 10 percent to the Lord) when I was just five-years-old. As a result, God has blessed and prospered my financial situation in so many ways that I can't take time to list them.

The rewards of taking God seriously over this have been many. In my life, job promotions and return on investments have gone way beyond my own wisdom and ability. I wholeheartedly suggest that you find out what God says about tithing.

Concerning finances, the questions I ask our people are as follows: "Do you believe in this church enough to stand with us financially?" "Do you find integrity in this church?" "Can you trust the leadership?" "Do you appreciate the results of our ministry?" "Do you care enough to support the ministries that flow from this church like water from a spring?" "Is this the principal place where your soul is fed?"

If the answers come up yes, then this church should be the principal focus of your giving pattern. Many people align themselves with a local church but at the same time get enthralled with the glamour of one of the various "media ministries." They attend their local church and benefit from its ministry. However, they focus their giving on some other organization because it seems large and successful.

In the end, you should support those who will stand over your grave and minister to your family when you are gone.

You should focus your giving on the ministry that is your first line of defense in your own struggle against Satan. This is why the Bible tells us to bring the tithe into the "storehouse" (Malachi 3:10-11). The storehouse in Old Testament days was a warehouse or granary from which the people were fed. The principle is as true today as it was when God spoke through the prophet Malachi. God wants us to invest in his spiritual granary "so there can be food in my house, says the Lord."

5. *Are you willing to serve God . . . without restraint?*

"Without restraint." I can't know what those words mean to you. Only God can speak to your heart and direct you into significant ministry. Hope Chapel is a ministry team. The leaders are like coaches and the members are players on the field. The New Testament teaches that "Their responsibility is to equip God's people to do his work" (Ephesians 4:12). Those leaders put their hearts into the equipping process. They do it well. Results in your own life depend on whatever you are willing to bring into the game. Will you lay everything on the line for God, or will you hold back? Achievement lays in the answer to that question.

God will call you to minister to your own family. He will probably call you to serve your immediate neighbors or perform some function within your own church. He may even call you to serve as a pastor or missionary. Rest assured he never calls us to do anything without making the task desirable. Are you available?

Serving God is costly. It consumes time, energy and even money. Surrender is a powerful theme throughout the Scriptures. A parting example of personal surrender is found in the life of Moses. The Bible tells us:

> It was by faith that Moses, when he grew up, refused to be treated as the son of Pharaoh's daughter. He chose to share the oppression of God's people instead of enjoying the fleeting pleasures of sin. He thought it was better to suffer for the sake of the Messiah than to own the treasures of Egypt, for he was looking ahead to the great reward that God would give him (Hebrews 11:24-26).

What a choice! The man grew up in a palace and was educated toward an important position in government. What made him think he had a better shot at improving the lot of the Israelis through personal activism than from a government job? It could only be the Spirit of the Lord.

Granted, he acted in his own anger on the day he beat up the Egyptian. God never gave him a license to kill. But it would be easy to fasten our eyes on the violence and fail to see that by intervention he marked himself as an Israeli. By getting involved, Moses chose to leave Pharaoh's family and embrace his own people. The Spirit of the Lord was already at work in his heart. He surrendered the ring of life-charting control.

Moses might have lived his life as a government official in Egypt. With luck, he may have even made some footnote on the pages of history. Almost certainly he would have remained rich and powerful. He intentionally gave up all the power and wealth that the world offered for the uncertainty of following Jehovah. But Moses is more than a footnote. He is the leader God chose for one of the most miraculous sequences of all time, the Exodus. He is also regarded as the father of most western legal codes. Beyond all that, if he were interested in power, playing number two to the Lord in the desert was pretty high up the chain of command. Had he refused God on the day the bush burned, he would have missed one of the greatest adventures of all time. Moses surrendered at the right time to the proper Master. And, he never regretted it.

I am writing all this to lead into a question. What will *you* do when the Lord asks you to let go of the ring and give him the reins of your life? I hope you will give him everything he asks.

The Best of
Ralph Moore

These audio tape albums are some of the best of Ralph Moore's teaching series. For more information on and **free samplings** of these teachings, and to order, log on to our website at **www.hopechapel.com**.

Stress Busting: Restoring My Soul — a series on worship
Comprehending Love & Marriage
In God We Trust: Making Your Money Work For You
Defeating Debt
Tough Questions About the Bible
10 Tools for Helping Friends Find God
Come Grow With Us
Winning in Tough Times
How to Remodel Your Spiritual Home
What's the Plan?

 STRAIGHT STREET PUBLISHING
A ministry of Hope Chapel Kaneohe
■
P.O. Box 240041
Honolulu, HI 96824-0041
■
1-800-711-9369 or 1-808-235-5814
Tuesday through Friday, 9 a.m. to 5 p.m.
Email: hopechapel@hopechapel.com
Website: www.straightstreet.com

Let Go of the Ring
by Ralph Moore
$13.95 • Paperback

Letting go is difficult, but it is the only way to success. This book chronicles the story of Hope Chapel and Ralph Moore's struggle to give God the "ultimate authority" in his life. And how, when he finally "let go of the ring," his ministry was so greatly blessed. It's also a book about friendship and values. We highly recommend it to young pastors and church planters. The values detailed throughout the book provide a frame on which to build your ministry philosophy and a great tool to reinforce those values with a budding leadership team.

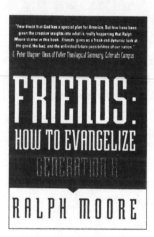

Friends: How to Evangelize Generation X
by Ralph Moore
$13.95 • Paperback

This is a "must read" especially for the Boomer pastor who is leading a church with very different values and needs from his own. It was written for three intensive purposes: (1) To motivate church leaders to understand that the future depends on their success with Generation X; (2) To press for building relationships as opposed to the tendency of using new programs to reach this particular generation; and (3) To provide some tools necessary to do the job. Ralph Moore, senior pastor of Hope Chapel Kaneohe, invites and challenges the Boomer church to cross the generational barrier and begin mentoring leaders from Generation X to carry the church and society beyond the next quarter century. Among the topics covered: Understanding rising movements of revival; what history and the Bible say about our responsibility to the next generation; who is Gen X and how they see their world; how to plant a Gen X church; and how to transition a Baby Boomer church to a Gen X church.

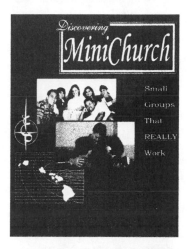

Discovering MiniChurch: Small Groups That Really Work
by Ralph Moore
only $69.95

Do you have an equipping model in your church to nurture relationships and disciples? This dynamic series will provide the tools required to meet the expectations and demands of today's church and the future. With practical, proven techniques, "Discovering MiniChurch" will help you lead your congregation to a deeper understanding and commitment in their relationship with Christ. You'll also receive pastoral tools that will not only increase your effectiveness, but ease the tremendous burdens you face as a leader of your ministry. *Includes six audio cassettes and 41-page workbook.*

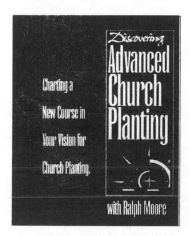

Discovering Advanced Church Planting
by Ralph Moore
only $89.95

A one-of-a-kind resource designed for you — pioneer pastors and church planters. In this breakthrough training series, Ralph Moore will not only provide you with the "nuts and bolts" of church planting, but will also give you the not-so-obvious insights that come from a seasoned and experienced "church planter." He'll take you beyond the step-by-step approach most church planting resources provide and guide you through the difficult relational issues all church planters have to deal with. "Discovering Advanced Church Planting" provides a wealth of information and wisdom that could save you months of frustration. *Includes eight audio cassettes and 54-page workbook.*

TO ORDER • 800.711.9369 • 808.235.5814 • www.straightstreet.com

How to Hire, Fire and Manage In-Between
by Ralph Moore
$69.95

This tape series is specifically designed to expand the ability of a pastor to recruit, train, hire, manage, and sometimes fire, both volunteer and paid staff. These six teachings and 24-page outline of notes also provide direct and essential insight to the requirements for working with Generation X. If you find yourself thinking: "I can't seem to find leaders who want to take the ball and run with it," or "Generation X sure has a different take on work and commitment than what I grew up with," you are not alone. Any senior pastor who is actively reaching out to Generation X can relate to the issues you're dealing with. In this tape series, you will learn how to build your "dream team" for the new millennium. Pastor Ralph Moore identifies six critical skill areas that need to be developed by today's pastor:

• How to Spot Holy Spirit Potential in Our People
• Raising Leaders Through Succession Management
• How to Hire Effectively
• Six Tools for Managing Paid Staff
• How to Deliver an Effective Reprimand
• How to Fire, When Forced

Stress Busting: Restoring My Soul
(a series on worship)
by Ralph Moore
$19.95

What does being worried, stressed out or de-pressed have to do with our worship time with God? In this 4-part teaching, you will learn that worship is infinitely more than just a "fill-in time" to adjust for latecomers before the pastor starts his teaching. Topics covered: Holding my soul in my hands; singing against depression and fear; teaching myself to worship (guest speaker: Ka'ala Souza); and never neglecting my soul.

10 Tools for Helping Friends Find God
by Ralph Moore
$19.95

In these powerful teachings you will learn 10 very simple tools that will help you share your faith without fear. Pastor Ralph draws from his own experience and a wealth of Bible knowledge in these tapes. His stories will warm your heart and show you how to enjoy the process of bringing friends to the Lord. In four, funny and instructive lessons you will learn: Why faith is "caught, not taught;" why hanging out with a mix of Christians and non-Christians results in people finding God; how to simply tell of your own spiritual journey; the power of "gossiping" about God and what He's done for your friends; how prayer can be the best tool for interactive evangelism; the tremendous advantage of building on shared viewpoints; the secret of asking tough questions of those questioning God; four basic Scriptures which present the whole Gospel; and how to move from hard questions to biblical answers.

Tough Questions About the Bible
by Ralph Moore
$19.95

Many people have hard questions about the Bible. Some are "professional skeptics" who delight in baiting Christians into hostile debates. But most are honest people looking for a reason to believe in God. Some are Christians who are not yet sure of their faith. This teaching series offers simple, reasonable answers to tough biblical questions. Using everyday language and humorous stories, Pastor Ralph offers "highly repeatable" answers to the following questions:
- How can you put so much trust in a man-made book?
- Why do you believe the Bible when you don't even have the original version?
- Why trust a book so filled with contradictions and mistakes?
- What makes you think the Bible is any better than other great religious books?

In God We Trust: Making Your Money Work For You
by Ralph Moore
$19.95

Meet the challenge of putting yourself in a relationship with God where He is responsible for your needs. By allowing Him to take control of your finances, you will reap the benefits of spiritual blessings! These keys are taught in a four-part series: How to get money without loving it; how to spend money without wasting it; how to tithe without regretting it; and how to tithe without fearing it

Comprehending Love and Marriage
by Ralph Moore
$59.95

Here in this one album of 12 teachings, Pastor Ralph Moore presents a classic series on a topic that strikes at the heart of people and relationships. Through thought-provoking and biblically-based teachings, Pastor Ralph will help you meet your most basic needs. Topics include:

- Collecting that "perfect" specimen (or, will the glass slipper really fit?) and what really happens when you marry
- Living together and other fantasies
- The perfect marriage (or, marriage as it was meant to be)
- That authority "thing" (resolving conflicts successfully, why marriages fail or succeed, and spiritual intimacy)
- Calming our fears (what is feared most in relationships, steps to overcoming relationship fears, and stages of recovery)
- Don't marry a loser
- True love or loving truly (how to know if you're in love, the myth of romantic love, finding the love of your life, and passionate love)
- Counterfeit versus compatibility
- Married to an unbeliever
- Unfortunately single (widowed or divorced)
- The second time around (remarriage when appropriate)